T0368586

Ancient Healings, Modern Miracles

How 3,000 Year Old Methods are Transforming the Lives of

Ordinary People in the 21st Century

By

Dawn Ressel

Foreword by Carla Weis, M.D.

© 2022 Dawn Ressel. All rights reserved.

No part of this book may be reproduced, stored in a retrieval system, or transmitted
by any means without the written permission of the author.

AuthorHouse™
1663 Liberty Drive
Bloomington, IN 47403
www.authorhouse.com
Phone: 833-262-8899

Because of the dynamic nature of the Internet, any web addresses or links contained in
this book may have changed since publication and may no longer be valid. The views
expressed in this work are solely those of the author and do not necessarily reflect the views
of the publisher, and the publisher hereby disclaims any responsibility for them.

Any people depicted in stock imagery provided by Getty Images are models,
and such images are being used for illustrative purposes only.
Certain stock imagery © Getty Images.

This book is printed on acid-free paper.

ISBN: 978-1-6655-7111-1 (sc)
ISBN: 978-1-6655-7110-4 (e)

Library of Congress Control Number: 2022917325

Print information available on the last page.

Published by AuthorHouse 09/30/2022

authorHOUSE®

About the Stories in this Book

All of the stories and people in this book are real. The names of clients have been changed and some identifying details altered to protect the privacy of the people we've had the privilege of working with.

In some cases, the story is told in first person by a certified Guide with The Modern Mystery School who is telling their own story. In the remaining cases, the stories are told in third person by the practitioner. For example, when it says, "the client came to me" - the "me" is the practitioner – either me or one of the contributors.

I wish to thank all of my clients and the clients of the contributors. I hope their stories enrich your life as much as they have enriched ours.

About the Advice in this Book

This book contains the direct experience and ideas of the author and contributors. It is intended to share the results that we have witnessed through our work with the ancient modalities described in this book.

Although anyone may find the guidance, practices, and understandings in this book to be useful, it is made available with the understanding that neither the author or the contributors are engaged in presenting specific medical, psychological, emotional, or spiritual advice. Nor is anything in this book intended to be a recommendation, diagnosis, prescription, or cure for any specific kind of medical, psychological, emotional or spiritual problem.

Each person has unique needs, and this book cannot take these individual differences into account. Each person should engage in a program of prevention, treatment, cure, or practice for their health situations only in consultation with a licensed, physician, therapist, or other qualified professional.

Dedication

To every person who knows they can do more, be more, and is worth more, but is lost in the storm and is struggling to find the way out. I was once you. May this book play a part in magnifying the spark of hope that resides within you. May that spark be the light within that guides you home to your true divine self.

Acknowledgements

I'd like to thank all of the people who have worked to preserve the methods of the lineage of King Salomon over many millennia. These methods have dramatically changed my life, the lives of those featured in this book, and the lives of so many others. I'd like to thank Founder Gudni Gudnason of The Modern Mystery School for making these tools broadly available to the public. Thank you to the Third Order for working tirelessly to keep these methods pure and sacred. Thank you to the Council of 12 Goddesses for your service and embodiment of the divine feminine.

Thank you to all the teachers who have helped me with my progression and healing journey, most notably, my Ritual Master teacher Ipsissimus Dave Lanyon and my Universal Hermetic Ray Kabbalah teacher Dr. Theresa Bullard-Whyke. Thank you to Erin Wallace for your mentorship and kindness. Thank you to Sandy Szabat for being my first Guide monitor and a stellar example of what it means to be a Guide in this lineage.

Thank you to Vanessa Nova and Rachel Miller for reflecting back my potential as an author. Thank you to Ariela Wilcox for helping make this book a reality. Thank you to Julia Tiffin for your personal angel reading that helped infuse this creation process with more light. Thank you to my peers and friends in The Modern Mystery School who have supported and inspired me along the way. Thank you to my family for your support over the years. Thank you to my clients for entrusting me to play a part in your healing journey. Thank you to the Hierarchy of Light and all beings of light who helped me bring this book to fruition. Thanks be to God.

Advance Praise for Ancient Healings, Modern Miracles

"The King Salomon lineage and mystery school tradition has perfected the art and science of healing in body, soul, and spirit. Today, we are fortunate enough to live in a time where we can gain access to these ancient methods and teachings that have stood the test of time, through the millennia. They show us that miracles are possible -- bringing hope, healing, and an openness to the power of real magick in our lives. The stories shared in this book are but a few of the real-life examples of such magick and miracles. Inspiring, hopeful, and empowering! The power to choose a life of healing and a more fulfilling life is in your hands!"
- Dr. Theresa Bullard, Ph.D. Physicist, Host of Mystery Teachings on Gaia TV, and International Instructor with The Modern Mystery School

"This book provides tremendous hope for those who are suffering, and reminds us that it's never too late to move forward. Each story offers a window to higher light, showing us how amazing life can be when we live aligned with our spirit."
- Sean Carey, D.C.

"As a medical doctor I am so grateful to see this book take fruition. Modern medicine, while crucial to our wellbeing, simply does not have all the answers. Human beings are much more than the physical body. And as our metaphysical knowledge reaches the masses, it is my wish to see each individual take responsibility for their own healing guided by their own self-knowledge & self-realization. This work is essential to that end."
- Dr. Ann Donnelly, MB MRCGP, Medical Doctor, Best Selling Author, Guide, Healer & International Teacher with The Modern Mystery School

"If you've been looking for that elusive "something" that can help transport you forward on your spiritual journey, or simply in life, then look no further than the amazing and very real personal stories compiled in this book. It may be exactly what you've been looking for!"
- Carla Weis, M.D.

Table of Contents

Foreword

Hello. My name is Carla Weis. I am a daughter, sister, mother, doctor and grandmother. I am also a Practitioner, Teacher and Guide in the Modern Mystery School.

It is such an honor for me to greet you here at the entrance to a world of magick! You are about to get a very intimate glimpse into the lives of people who have found their way out of various life struggles and into lives filled with recovery, hope, fulfillment, and joy!

That may sound like a familiar tagline these days, but there is a huge difference here. The path these people took on their healing journey was that of the Modern Mystery School, which holds the ancient lineage of King Salomon and is one of 7 mystery schools on the planet today. This school has existed for thousands of years. It's the school of Aristotle and Plato, Leonardo DaVinci, Joan of Arc, Shakespeare, Nikola Tesla, Carl Jung, David Bowie and Carlos Santana as well as many others – including the people in this book! The reality is that for most of humanity's existence on this planet, these tools and ancient wisdom teachings used for supporting the evolution of humanity were not available to the average person. Today, they are. And that's because in 1997, a man by the name of Gudni Gudnason, an Ipsissimus and lineage key holder, founded the Modern Mystery School. Before then, all of this existed "behind the curtain." Remember the famous line from The Wizard of Oz? The voice said, "Pay no attention to the man behind the curtain." Well, it's time to pay attention!

I was moved to tears so many times as I read the stories in this book. My tears flowed from a heart that was filled with compassion and gratitude for the ability of these people to transform themselves and their lives. And, for the fact that this kind of transformation is possible! These people chose to use the tools of a tried-and-true path of progression that no worldly system can offer. That's right. I said no worldly system. Because we are all in this world, but we are not of it. And neither is this path. These people overcame their challenges using ancient tools, God-given tools, that exist for us to grow and move forward in life, to improve and evolve, to find our way and indeed to master the maze of life. This is what real magick is. The "k" stands for keys because real magick holds keys, keys for life. The Modern Mystery School is a real magick school! It is now operating in over 60 countries with multiple headquarters around the world. Our mission quite simply is World Peace.

I will not expand on my own story but suffice it to say that I am a medical doctor (neonatologist), a mother of five daughters, and grandmother of four – so far. I have always loved life and people. Before I began my exploration of the Modern Mystery School, my life was good. I was in service to humanity. I was happy and I felt fulfilled in my life purpose. But I was always seeking for more knowledge, more enlightenment and more answers to the eternal questions of life that we all eventually ask: "Why am I here? What's the meaning of life? And death?". I found my way to the Modern Mystery School and followed the yellow brick road awhile, waiting to find the end of the road so I could move on to the next thing, and you know what I found? There can always be more! More fulfillment, more love, more joy. Life can just keep getting better! My service to humanity expanded. And I did find answers to those elusive life questions. And I also found that with more answers, come more questions. And if you want to explore eternal questions, the answers are – you guessed it – eternal. And in my exploration, and in service to others' explorations, I have found great fulfillment and great joy.

In our world today, there are so many people who are quietly suffering, quietly allowing the voice of their souls to disappear. But there is hope. There is always hope. They <u>can</u> find healing, joy, and fulfillment. We all can. Healing is possible. A better life is possible. If you need proof in real-world stories, this book is full of them!

What <u>is</u> healing? We can heal our body, but we can also heal our soul. We can make progress in the physical life, but we can also make progress in our spiritual life. As humans, our "self" is both physical and spiritual, and our DNA holds the codes for both. Healing therefore must be applied to all of it! As a medical doctor who is also a spiritual guide in this ancient lineage, I understand this. The goal is to strike a balance in maintaining the health of <u>all</u> of you. Your physical body matters and your soul body matters. Everything that we work with in the Modern Mystery School connects us to the nature of our soul, and helps us to heal it, while we are here in the physical. And as we heal our soul, it is always reflected in our physical life. Many of us understand the importance of physical body health. What have you done for your soul lately? In truth, we heal ourselves. Our healing happens through our own efforts, our own choices. What choices are you making? Maybe one of the stories in this book will help you to make a choice that leads to your own healing.

As we heal, we begin to feel more contentment, happiness and joy. And when we can express more contentment, happiness and joy, it gives others hope. And hope can make all the difference! You know, people say doctors save lives. The truth is that anyone can save a life. Even a book can save a life. Maybe this one will save yours. Maybe one of these stories will remind you of someone you know, and you can share it with them. Sometimes we don't know what to say, but you can just give them this book and say, "Maybe you'll find some inspiration in here. I did."

Maybe you've already had some experience with the Modern Mystery School and maybe you haven't, but either way this book lets us see a far bigger picture of what's possible! So, share it. And if you do have experience with the Modern Mystery School healings, activations and initiations, I'm <u>sure</u> you will share it!

I would like to acknowledge Dawn Ressel for following her own inspiration to put this book together. In doing so, she has done a great service. And to all those who bravely contributed to this amazing collection, I sincerely salute your efforts to serve yourself first and save your own life. And last, but not least, I sincerely pay great homage to Founder Gudni Gudnason, a truly great man who answered the divine call to open this ancient and royal lineage to the public in 1997, and to the other men of the illustrious Third Order, Ipsissimus Dave Lanyon and Ipsissimus Hideto Nakagome, and the women on the Council of 12, who all humbly and tirelessly serve to ensure that this great effort remains true and pure in its service to all of humanity. Otherwise, it would be just another set of healing modalities in just another self-help program, just another seminar company to bolster your self-confidence and motivation. Yes, these things may assist you in recovering, healing and improving your life, but what of your soul? Isn't there always something still missing? What of the meaning of your life beyond this life? What if you could find true fulfillment and joy at a soul level? That is the beauty of this book. It opens your mind to that very possibility.

So, I invite you to open your mind to what's possible as you turn these pages. Look at the table of contents and find the stories in this book that <u>you</u> can relate to. While no one is exactly like you, reading about someone else who has been in a similar situation always helps. Let the stories in this book move you to find your way, to <u>your</u> path, to a life that you once dreamed of.

These pages allow you to peek into that magickal place where the human soul – and indeed humanity - can heal and evolve into the highest version of itself.

And as we heal ourselves, we find that we are in a better place to serve others. And as we help others to heal, we open our minds to a unity consciousness, and so the world then has more unity. As we heal ourselves, we heal the world.

This book is about healing. It's about hope. It's about us; it's about humans trying to find our way on this planet we call Earth—finding our way to unity and peace.

And when you make the choice to pull back that curtain, you will see that the wizard is YOU!

So be the wizard and create magick in your life! In fact, that is exactly what we are supposed to be doing!

Magickally yours,
Carla Morris Weis, MD
Huntington Beach, CA

Introduction

We were lying in bed that night in 2014, like many other nights before. He was silent while I rambled on angrily about my many frustrations. That night he responded with, "You keep talking about all the same things over and over. You're really angry. Maybe you should get some help."

The man was my ex-husband. And he usually remained silent while I ranted. Listening or not listening, I can't say. But it was rare for him to give any response. And he wasn't really the type to suggest "getting help." His words jolted me into reality.

"He's right," I thought. I was on the verge of a nervous breakdown. I had no idea how to get out of the hamster wheel. I didn't know how to escape the repetitive angry thoughts, the resentment of things present and past. But I was so tired of my own bullshit. After suffering from generalized anxiety disorder since childhood, I was finally ready for a solution.

I grew up in a small town of Spring Hill, Florida about an hour north of Tampa on the coast of the Gulf of Mexico. I am the oldest of three girls. My parents were 18 and 25 years old when I was born.

From a young age, I was given a lot of responsibility. I can pinpoint the moment when the burden of responsibility turned me into a very serious child. It was when my middle sister was diagnosed with Type 1 diabetes.

Around the age of eight, I was trained to know all the ways my sister might end up in mortal danger. I knew the protocol – who to call, what signs to look for, how to prevent her from unwittingly putting herself into a diabetic coma or missing an insulin shot. My Mom tried to teach me how to give her a shot in case of emergency. But truth be told, I just couldn't make myself do it.

And then one day around the age of nine, my preparation was tested. My sister went into a diabetic coma. I was the one who found her. I was the one who called for the ambulance. I was the one who tried to get orange juice and sugar down her throat while she was unconscious. I watched as they pulled her out of the house on a stretcher, not knowing if she would live or die.

Thankfully my sister recovered, and she is still with us today. She is a mother and even a grandmother. But the damage that event did on my psyche was permanent. A few years ago in a meditation session, I realized that the root of many issues I'd had stemmed from that day. I had not forgiven myself or my parents for the events that unfolded. I was holding onto so much anger and shame that manifested in a variety of self-sabotaging patterns.

This is just one vignette from my childhood, but I believe this event and other situations in my childhood were the root of my generalized anxiety disorder. I was hypervigilant. I never felt safe. I was always on the lookout for something tragic to happen.

Before I even realized that I had anxiety disorder, I used to think, "This is just how life is. And this is how it will always be. Those people who seem happy are all just pretending." I wasn't as good at pretending as them. That was how I rationalized it. I simply couldn't imagine a life without a constant pit in my stomach, without constant worries that something horrible is about to happen. Without imagining the worst possible outcome of every scenario. Without the obsessive thoughts steeped in resentment about all the ways I believed other people had wronged me.

So back to the jolting statement that "I should get help." I took his advice. I started searching fervently on the internet for a solution. Somehow I knew I needed to escape my life for a time period and just get away. I started looking for retreats. I searched the internet for weeks, finding things and quickly dismissing them. I knew I would know when I found it. The first few weeks nothing I found seemed right, from silent retreats to mindfulness retreats to yoga. I just kept thinking, "Sure, I'll feel better during the retreat, but then I'll go home and nothing will change." I was looking for lasting results.

And then I found it. Looking back, I would call it the sledgehammer of inner child healing retreats. But it was what I needed right then. I needed something dramatic. I was so deep and far gone. I was so desperate. I found the website of this retreat deep in the bowels of the interweb. Their webpage was very basic, but on the homepage it had a checklist. It said, "Does this sound like you? We can help." There were ten points, and I checked all of them. The retreat cost $4,000, but I didn't hesitate. My spiritual guides were giving me very clear signals. This is it! I called the next day to register.

No doubt that retreat made a huge impact. It was the start I needed for my healing journey. It helped, but in the way a sledgehammer does. It helped me clear a lot, but it also left a mess in its wake. It showed me just how broken I was and how much more work I had to do.

In that retreat I was introduced to meditation and spirituality without dogma. I was introduced to the concept of Higher Self for the first time. I did meditation in earnest for the first time. I felt the potential of spiritual connection in a way I hadn't before.

I was raised Christian. I was exposed to a number of churches in my childhood, from Baptist to Catholic, to non-denominational, to Pentecostal. The part of church I remember liking was the feeling of reverence and holiness. And I always felt very connected to the actual teachings of Jesus Christ. But when it got to the sermons about fire and brimstone, I shut down. None of that sat well with me. I didn't believe that humans were inherently evil or that God was punishing us.

I didn't believe that the God I felt connected with when I stepped into a holy space would leave any of us behind. I did not believe God looked down on us. When I heard the actual words of Jesus Christ they felt kind, loving, accepting, and gentle. In contrast to the fire and brimstone sermons, it all felt very dissonant. Eventually I became disillusioned by Christianity. And yet I left the door open to the possibility that a God I would someday connect with does exist.

Then I married a staunch atheist. He would become adversarial even at the mention of anything to do with religion or spirituality. So I put aside my own desire to experience the divine. It felt much easier than to cause a rift in our marriage. My deep fear of being alone overruled a spiritual quest.

After the retreat, I got back into therapy and got on medication to lessen my anxiety. I got mild relief from those methods. They helped me survive, but not thrive. I had no hope of a full recovery.

A friend I met at the retreat introduced me to Soka Gakkai Buddhist chanting. I was finally at a place where I felt strong enough in myself to ignore my ex-husband's feelings about my spiritual journey. I just started doing it. And the couple years I practiced, I got good results. But the growth I experienced created a distance between me and my husband that I couldn't see being reconciled. I had outgrown the need for a co-dependent marriage.

My soul was screaming at me! I knew I had a big mission to fulfill. I didn't know yet what it was, but I knew that I had to break out of the box of that marriage in order to fulfill it. My connection with my spirit guides and Higher Self had gotten to the point that I trusted them enough to take the leap. I asked for a divorce.

Now I do not assign blame to my ex-husband. That is not what this is about, because I co-created that reality. It is simply about two people who once made sense together growing apart. He was a good man. I am forever grateful that he gave me the nudge that prompted my healing journey. He supported me through many years when I felt I simply couldn't do it on my own. But when I could do it on my own, the bonds of marriage started to feel like a prison. And I was the warden. Those were the exact words I said to my therapist.

Before I started healing, I made all of my major life decisions from a place of fear. Fear of the unknown, fear of poverty, fear of a major disaster, etc. My marriage was like a child's security blanket. Once I started becoming an emotional and spiritual adolescent, it was time to let go.

After my divorce, I started socializing a lot more. That was when I met my future Guide with The Modern Mystery School. We met at a potluck that I somehow knew I needed to be at. I was invited to the potluck by an acquaintance. The potluck was 45 minutes away from my house, and I had to leave work early and travel through rush hour traffic. It would have been very easy to ignore this invite as it was inconvenient. Yet something strong was pulling me to this event. As I was eating, a woman I never met before sat right across from me and starting talking about her amazing healing journey from all kinds of physical and mental illnesses. She said that because of all of the healing she received, she became an energy healer in the same lineage.

Nothing this woman said when we met made any logical sense to me. Her claims sounded fantastical! Energy healing, King Salomon and healing miracles were so far outside my sphere of awareness at that time. I was a "successful" middle manager at a software company, making very good money, working a "normal" full-time job. And yet my soul knew she was telling the truth! I was fascinated by her and everything she said. I knew this woman had answers and I needed to know her. I knew I really needed more healing, and I held out hope that perhaps she was the person that was going to lead the way. Meeting her was the beginning of my healing journey that I describe in my story in Chapter One.

Soon after meeting her, I received an ancient healing called the Life Activation. And after that, I went to a profound workshop called the Empower Thyself Initiation. These two things together changed my life entirely.

I am writing this book six years after I completed these two steps. And I've taken many more steps since then. Nothing about my life is the same. I have completely healed of generalized anxiety disorder. And the miracles go well beyond that. I never in a million years could have imagined the life I have today. A life of joy. A life of wonder. A life of purpose. A courageous life motivated by passion and purpose, not fear. A life as a certified Healer, Teacher, and Guide with The Modern Mystery School.

This book is a collection of stories, including mine, about the profound shifts people have experienced through working with The Modern Mystery School. It is the lineage of King Salomon. King Salomon was the king of Israel from 970-931 BCE. He was the second son of King David. King David used the sword to resolve conflicts. King Salomon wanted a different way. He prayed to God for wisdom, which was granted. It allowed him to become a peaceful king. The teachings and healing modalities of this lineage go back over 3,000 years unbroken and have remained pure and intact that time. That is what it means to say it is unbroken.

Most of those 3,000 years these powerful methods were kept fairly secret, available only to royalty or priests and priestesses. They were protected from persecution, distortion, or being lost forever by brave men and women who vowed to keep them safe until humans were ready for them to be made available broadly. That time is now.

King Salomon predicted there would be a time on the planet when people were ready for these tools. A time when a mass awakening was not only possible, but probable, and even more likely with the aid of these tools.

I've collected these stories because I know how impactful these methods are. I know how many people truly need them and are seeking; they just haven't found them yet. I have seen the miraculous results in my own life and the lives of others. These stories come from me, my clients, my colleagues, and their clients.

I'm sharing these stories because I feel a responsibility to make more people aware of solutions that can literally save lives. There are so many "solutions" out there, yet the problems are only growing. Anxiety disorder is the most prevalent mental health crisis of our time. And I myself have overcome it.

I've been on both sides, so I am in a perfect position to talk about it. I believe the gap for people's problems of many varieties can be filled by something they haven't yet tried: ancient spiritual healings that have stood the test of time. In this book, I invite you to go on a journey with me to learn about people from all walks of life who are experiencing modern miracles as a result of these ancient tools. You might even see yourself or your loved ones in these stories. And if so, it may bring hope that there are solutions out there to help overcome the obstacles you are facing.

One: Mental Healing

Man's task is to become conscious of the contents that press upward from the unconscious. As far as we can discern, the sole purpose of human existence is to kindle a light in the darkness of mere being.

- Carl Jung

Dawn's Story: Healed Overnight of Generalized Anxiety Disorder
By Dawn Ressel

I used to feel powerless. I suffered most of my life with generalized anxiety disorder, as well as several phobias. I was consumed with fear. My mind was cluttered with "what if" scenarios where I inevitably imagined the worst possible outcome to any situation. Even minor inconveniences or deviations from my plan could set me into a tailspin. On the outside, I looked successful by society's standards. I got a Master's Degree. I landed great jobs, earned promotions, and ended up making a lot of money. Yet on the inside, I was a house of cards. I could barely hold it together. I had mastered my intellect well enough, but my emotions were like a raging hurricane, and I was completely disconnected from my heart.

I recall a time when my ex-husband and I went for a weekend trip to Julian, California. Julian is a quaint mountain town known for its apple pie. It was meant to be a quick, relaxing getaway. However, once we got there on a Saturday it was quite busy and difficult to find parking. With each passing minute, I was getting more and more anxious. Until my anxiety boiled over. After about 10 minutes of circling around, Ted turned right at the stop sign, and I snapped at him. "Why didn't you go left? We already went this way! I don't know why you can't find a stupid parking spot!" Our weekend getaway quickly went from relaxing to super stressful over something this small. This vignette basically summed up my life with anxiety disorder. The littlest of challenges seemed like mountains. And one small setback could ruin my entire day – or a weekend vacation.

I would get upset by what other people said very easily. I got angry and offended often. Social media was basically a minefield for me. It could change my emotional state very easily if someone said "the wrong" thing. And the gamut of what I considered "wrong" was pretty wide. I was not in control of my own emotions. I was easily thrown off balance. I was afraid to drive almost anywhere besides to and from work, which was a necessity. I would often have panic attacks if I had to drive an unfamiliar route.

In 2009, I started seeing a therapist for the first time. I knew there was something wrong with me, but I didn't realize how much I was actually suffering. After a few sessions my therapist diagnosed me with:

- Generalized anxiety disorder (meaning you're anxious for no particular reason – it doesn't even need a trigger)
- Several phobias including fear of heights, fear of driving, and mild agoraphobia
- Panic disorder that was triggered by exposure to one or more of my phobias

I continued therapy and eventually got onto medication to help curb it. My experience with the medication was that it did ease the anxiety somewhat, but it also flattened my overall emotional range. I felt quite zombie-like on it. But I thought it was better than the alternative.

The combination of my mild agoraphobia (the irrational fear of leaving home) and the shame I had around my anxiety led me to isolate myself. I was so afraid of what people might think of me if they knew I couldn't do the most basic of things, such as drive on the highway. I had no real friends other than co-workers. My ex-husband was the only person I trusted to see this side of me and not judge me.

After being on medication for a while, I had a visit with my psychiatrist who said, "If you ever feel like you don't need the medication anymore, call me and I'll help you wean off of it." And I remember sitting there thinking, "I'm never going to call you." I had absolutely zero hope that I would ever be well enough to not feel like I needed the medication.

In 2016, I had the Life Activation session. Almost immediately after the session I started to see the effects of my anxiety disorder lessen. Two weeks after the Life Activation, I went on a trip of a lifetime to Thailand. It was a solo trip. It was by far the most adventurous thing I had ever done. I had been planning it for months and was looking forward to it, but somehow I knew I should receive the Life Activation before the trip.

During the trip to Thailand, another side of me started to reveal itself. I was like a flower slowing unfurling her petals after the Life Activation. This was the most complicated travel I'd ever done, yet I wasn't stressed out. For the first time in my life, I was actually able to relax on vacation! I felt myself being in the moment. I was able to sink in and actually enjoy the beautiful nature and culture around me. This was very new for me!

Typically, on vacation I would be so worried about what was going to go wrong that I didn't enjoy myself. But this trip was totally different. I was fully present. I got to visit beautiful temples, relax at the beach, spend the night at an elephant sanctuary and bathe an elephant, visit the most beautiful orchid garden, hike alongside amazing waterfalls, go snorkeling at a coral reef, and take tours with an indigenous mountain tribe. I pushed myself physically and mentally when I went on a 16-mile bike ride through some jungle terrain that was a little bit dangerous to be honest! And yet I stayed calm, collected, and joyful the entire time.

Also after my Life Activation, I suddenly had the strong desire to have friends. I did something that would have been highly unusual and scary to me before that - I joined Meetup and started hosting potlucks at my house.

I had no idea who was going to show up to my house. It was a little bit crazy, but mostly brilliant. I met so many people by hosting these potlucks. I'm still friends with some people I met this way, and I learned a lot about myself by doing this.

I learned that I have several gifts that were completely forgotten and untapped. I have a gift for connecting with new people easily. I have a gift for making people feel welcome and at ease in my home and in my presence. I have a gift for holding space for people to open up and express themselves.

Turns out that I have interpersonal gifts that laid dormant because of my social anxiety. After my Life Activation, suddenly these gifts came to life and brought so much joy into my life as a result. The Life Activation started to awaken me to the potential of life being more than drudgery or something I have to struggle to get through.

In 2017, I decided to do the Empower Thyself Initiation through The Modern Mystery School. I decided to do it out of curiosity and a gut feeling that I was supposed to be there. It was the next step after the Life Activation, which after almost a year had proven itself to have increased my enjoyment of life. Yet I had no expectations of healing or anything dramatically changing as a result. So I was completely unprepared for what happened next.

The class itself was very healing. It helped me reconcile some of the issues I'd struggled with around religion. It helped me feel closer to God. It helped me understand my own power as a divine being, which I was never really taught in church. I got a lot out of the class, but I still didn't expect what happened at the initiation ceremony.

While I was being initiated, which happens at the very end of the class, I heard angels singing. Literally. It was in a language I could not understand. But it was absolutely beautiful. I looked around to see if I was imagining it, because it seemed so fantastical. But there was no explanation for this sound other than it was supernatural. Afterwards, I asked the other people in the class if they heard it. No one heard the singing except for me and the woman who initiated me. I couldn't believe it!

And if that sounds incredible, you won't believe what happened afterwards. A couple days after the initiation, I thought to myself, "Wait a minute. I don't have anxiety. And I haven't had it since initiation. What is going on?" That negative voice in my head that always told me to be afraid? Gone. That feeling of dread in the pit of my stomach that followed me everywhere? Gone. It was replaced by peace. Silence. To this day, I am anxiety disorder free. It had nothing to do with therapy or medication, which only gave me mild relief after many years. It was the Empower Thyself Initiation which completely healed me of anxiety disorder overnight.

Even at the worst of times in my life, I have never been called dumb or foolish. Anyone who knows me knows that I am analytical, rational, and practical. I only want things that work. And things that work repeatedly. That is what I have found with this lineage. Real, repeatable results. Every other initiate I know who's applied the tools has become a much better version of themselves.

Day one in this school you are told you are a divine being. And they keep reinforcing this, until one day you may finally believe it. They tell you that you have a unique and beautiful expression as that divine being. They tell you that you have a purpose that no one else on this planet can fulfill. It's your job to discover it!

They do not tell you have to believe certain things (dogma). They show you how to become. How to become who you really are and let go of the rest. They help you heal the traumas, let go of the masks, rid yourself of projections, tear down walls… anything that is getting in the way of your true expression and your true purpose.

It is an absolute miracle to me that, in only six years on this path, I have healed so much that I am now a spiritual Guide. That means I get to help others in their healing journey and spiritual path. I am fulfilling my highest purpose – the true reason why I am here on this planet, right here, right now!

I have a completely new life, filled with purpose, joy, and meaning. I am dedicated to service. My life is magickal! I connect with nature, animals, and plants in ways that I never thought possible. I practice Wicca/shamanic magick, which allows me to work with minerals, plants, and herbs to enhance my life. I see God in all things, great and small. God is in every aspect of our world from the practical to the highly spiritual, and I feel that connection. I've learned that the enjoyment of life is godly!

After really dedicating myself to this work, I know much more of who I am. I am a goddess. I am a healer. I am a divine being. I am unlike anyone else on this planet, and I do not want to be anyone else. I want to be me! I love me! The journey back home to know myself in this way is the most rewarding journey I've ever taken. And it keeps unfolding more and more with each day.

Lorraine's Story: From Childhood Near-Death to Flourishing Adult
By Lorraine Pimienta

My life started out like many others. I was born to a Mexican-American family, and we all lived in a small two-bedroom apartment in the suburbs of Los Angeles. My parents were so happy to have me -- and they made sure to take good care of me.

When I was 9 months old, my mother and I went to the pediatrician for a baby wellness check. While I was laying on the table, the doctor felt my abdomen, my mother noticed his expression turn very serious and he left the room. A few moments later, he returned to the room with a colleague who also felt my abdomen. The pediatrician picked me up and handed me back to my mother and said: "You need to take your baby to Children's Hospital Los Angeles right away. I have already called them to let them know you are coming."

In shock and panic, while holding me, my mother ran to her car and drove to our two bedroom apartment. It was too early for mobile phones, so after failing to reach my father who was substitute teaching at the time, she scribbled a note and left it on the front door for him to meet her at the hospital as quick as he could.

When we arrived, I was pulled from my mother's arms and I was swept away by a sea of doctors and nurses to be taken away for testing. My mother sat there alone and confused until my grandmother, my aunt, and my father later joined her as I went through CT Scans and bloodwork for days. Those days were a blur for my whole family, but at one point my mother noticed my name come up on the board at the hospital under the word tumor. I had no official diagnosis at this point, and the word tumor didn't mean anything to my mother and father. It was only a few days later when the doctors approached my family and said: "Your daughter has Wilm's Tumor Stage V", a childhood cancer of the kidneys.

From that point on, I went through many rounds of chemotherapy, had a catheter inserted into one of the major veins leading to my heart, and had multiple surgeries. Some of these were exploratory, where I was cut all the way across my abdomen from left to right leaving massive surgical scars. In one of those surgeries, I had my entire right kidney removed, along with the cancerous tumor threatening my life. After a few months of treatment, my parents were told that I had gone into remission and I was stopping chemotherapy. I was just 1 year old.

Life moved on. I still had multiple follow up trips to the hospital, but as I had been healthy for a few years my parents decided to have another baby. I am so grateful that my very first memory was meeting my brother for the first time, because my second memory was lying on the operating table, surrounded by people looking down at me wearing surgical masks and an oxygen mask being placed on my face. The cancer had returned, this time in my left kidney. I was only 3 years old when I had more surgeries where they removed 80% of my remaining kidney, had even more rounds of chemotherapy and this time I remember losing all of my hair.

My experience with this second round of cancer was really defined by my understanding of life in the few years I'd had on the Earth.

I thought the nurses who inserted chemotherapy into my hands were my friends as I saw them all the time. The other children with me in the cancer ward had bald heads just like me! I had adults visiting me at pre-school, at home, and at the hospital who would bring me stuffed animals, dolls, cupcakes, and balloons. I knew I would always be able to stand first in line at school, the teachers allowed me to play a little longer than the other children and I didn't have to clean up my toys. I knew I was treated a little differently than everyone else, and the three year old me thought I knew the reason why…. It's because I am super cute!!!!

After a few months, I had once again gone into remission, with less than perfect kidney function and life moved on. I continued to go to the hospital for follow up visits and accepted that this was my life; I didn't question it. These hospital appointments were routine and cancer was never discussed outside of the hospital at home.

It was when I was about to start high school that my family and I had a meeting with my doctor to discuss a kidney transplant. I didn't understand since I was 14 and felt pretty good. I was thin all over, but I was still ok. I was told I was anemic, and that got me out of Physical Education, which I was definitely ok with, but another surgery and more huge scars? I felt like I just couldn't do it! I went home, and I never talked to my Mom and Dad about what was discussed that day.

The 14 year old me was already very self-conscious about my surgical scars. And I hated that I had to add medicine to my school routine where some teachers would ask me some very personal questions. I loved that I was thin, because that was the beauty norm, but I buried and repressed the very idea that I was on the way to being added to the organ donation waiting list. I was about to go into some very important years where I wanted to be accepted by my peers and my body was about to really start failing me once again. There is such a shortage of organ donors that to even be accepted onto the waiting list, you need to hit a threshold of organ failure, even if you have the early warning signs like I did. My parents were too old to donate to me and my brother was too young, so I had to wait for a kidney.

In the years that followed, I tried to keep up with my peers and played high school water polo, but I was the worst on the team. I started to feel more and more tired during class and would have trouble paying attention. My brain started to become foggy and I began to lose my capacity for learning. I had a hard time standing up straight, and I lost my appetite completely. Walking long distances and being awake the whole day was impossible and my grades plummeted in school. Because of my failing grades, I lost privileges, including being able to park close to my high school. I remember my lungs heaving and my bones creaking as I struggled to climb the hill to my car.

Why didn't I say anything? I didn't want to be different. I didn't want to have kidney failure! I didn't speak about what was happening to me because no one could know and if I talked about it, then I would be admitting that organ failure was really happening to me! I wanted to be a normal teenager and to be like everyone else so badly. By not acknowledging what was happening to me and not having the skills to cope, I completely rejected myself and my reality, and that allowed room for self-hatred to seep into my life. I hated myself, and I hated my body.

The call for a kidney came when I was 18 years old, a month before I graduated from high school and just a few days before my high school prom. I was terrified. My father raced home to collect me, left a note to my mother on the microwave and we drove to the hospital. This time I knew exactly what was happening to me and I knew that I was going to go into life altering surgery.

The nurse practitioner told me, "Lorraine: this is the best graduation present you could ask for." But at the time, to me, it really didn't feel like it at all. I was going to miss my high school prom, and I wasn't going to get to wear my beautiful dress that I had custom made for me - as the

US size 0 was simply too big! Following the surgery and in the Intensive Care Unit, I remember tubes sticking out from different points of my body and looking at the clock and wondering what my school friends were doing. Where are they going to dinner, when they arriving to our prom venue, were they already dancing the night away while I stayed in that hospital bed?

Luckily for me, I made a friend while in the hospital, who had also had a kidney transplant a few years before and whose prom was in a few weeks. He asked me to go with him, and a few weeks later we attended Prom. Each day after I left the hospital I would stay awake longer and longer; I gained muscle mass that I didn't even know was possible; I got the boobs of my dreams; and one day a familiar yet foreign feeling hit me square in the stomach and I thought, "Oh! I think I'm hungry."

In the following months, the physical recovery was much smoother than the emotional and mental impact that having cancer twice and years of kidney failure had on me. I had severe PTSD and, like before, couldn't talk about what happened to me. I didn't want anyone to know that I had a kidney transplant and that I had been sick. I saw myself as damaged goods.

For years this mindset continued, and I was very shy and depressed. As I regained my physical health, I went through the motions of attending community college. I met my first great life and spiritual teacher who was my communications professor. She helped me realize that I was not damaged goods like I thought I was. In this classroom, I heard about The Modern Mystery School for the first time and met some of the initiates. I remember thinking there was something really different about the initiates, and I liked them a lot. It was as if the initiates could move through life more easily and freely than I could. At this point, I felt that I had been left completely battered by life, but the people who had worked with The Modern Mystery School weren't, and I wanted to be like them!

A few months later, while sitting in the classroom, a young woman came into the classroom who was a guest speaker and began talking about the Life Activation and the Emotional Cord Cutting. I KNEW I had a lot of cords, and contacted her shortly after her visit to book a cord cutting. As we spoke on the phone, she told me that she recommended a Life Activation over the cord cutting. I decided to trust her and go ahead with the Life Activation.

At this point in time, I had experienced Reiki and had only recently been introduced to energy work. I expected the Life Activation to be like Reiki, but it was completely different! After the session, my Guide told me that she was having a two-day workshop called Empower Thyself Initiation that was going to be taking place in a few short weeks. I wanted to study with the mystery school and asked her if I would be a part of it after the workshop. She confirmed I would, and I signed up right then and there and marked it in my calendar. That very night, I felt the huge changes in my mindset, and I wanted to re-evaluate what I allowed into my life when I saw my friends that evening. The Life Activation changed me right away.

I was so excited about the two day Empower Thyself Initiation, that I counted down the days until the weekend of the class arrived. In that class, I learned more about my energy field and how I could manage it better. I used the teachings and rituals I learned from the class every day and things shifted for me immediately. I was not the shy and depressed girl that I once was. I had a new-found bravery where I knew I could do anything with my life that I wanted, and a few months later I moved across the world to Europe to have an adventure.

At the time of writing this, 14 years have passed since attending the Empower Thyself Initiation and my life has changed completely very quickly. I got to live for the first time! I started working full time, I had my first boyfriend, I fell in love, I made friends from all over Europe, I danced in clubs around the world and stayed awake all night, I travelled across Europe, to the Middle East, Africa and Asia and I got to laugh until I cried. I was living!

The most wonderful thing from my healing and initiation in the Mystery School is that I have continued to grow, heal and year after year I feel stronger in myself and what I am meant to do in this life. My story has an unusual start, and there were times when I was younger that I didn't think I was ever going to be able to lead a joyful life. But with the incredible healings, activations and the initiatory path, I cannot wait to see what else life has in store!

Jeannie's Story: Healing Ancestral Depression
By Jeannie Vassos

I had a fairly normal, middle-class upbringing. I was considered a "good girl." I got good marks in school and didn't cause trouble in my teenage years. I got married at 21 and had two children before I turned 25. We worked hard and had a good life, the "millionaire's family" without the millions. We had a nice house, 2 cars, and yearly vacations. I was a stay-at-home mom for my children's early-childhood years, and then began working for the family business in property management which included a very flexible schedule. It all looked good on the surface, right? However, I would wake up in the morning and dread starting my day. Every interaction made me jumpy, and any social event made me want to crawl into a hole. I didn't know how to enjoy myself anymore because I questioned and doubted everything. While I loved my husband and children, my job wasn't difficult, and my life was "good", I felt empty inside. I had done all the "right" things, so why did I feel so bad? I felt unworthy of wanting more from life.

For the longest time, I knew something was wrong and that I needed help, but I didn't want to go down the medical route and take pharmaceutical drugs. Just like how I have never used alcohol, cigarettes, or drugs to make me feel better, because I knew they were only a temporary fix. So, I began to delve into many self-help books, classes, and therapy, then ventured into new age spirituality. It all was helpful. I began noticing my thoughts and when they were negative and bringing me down, I changed them to something positive. This helped tremendously, but I still couldn't get rid of the empty feeling.

Through my Reiki practitioner, I met a Guide with the Modern Mystery School who gave me an Emotional Cord Cutting and a Life Activation (2008). Immediately I knew something was different! I felt a sense of peace and calm that I had never experienced before, and unlike anything else I had tried, it stayed with me, along with new clarity, as though a fog had lifted. I finally had hope!

I began to see what I was avoiding in life, which had been causing the depression and emptiness. I also began questioning why I had made certain decisions in my life, and more accurately, who I had made them for, and not surprisingly, it wasn't for me. Although I didn't know what exactly had given me this peace, calm and clarity, I needed to know what else there was. My Guide provided a few healings and classes, but it wasn't until after attending the Empower Thyself Initiation that my life began to truly change.

At first, I was able to accomplish my daily home and work responsibilities faster and with more efficiency. This created more time and freedom for me to begin seeing what else life had to offer, whereas before I felt like I was stuck in a predestined box. My depression was greatly lifting and every day was better and better because I had faith that my future had unlimited potential.

This change was significant enough that my husband noticed and asked to receive the Life Activation for himself, and he also wanted our children to receive it (2010). They also received the Empower Thyself Initiation and our family life shifted incredibly. For all of us, life didn't seem so stressful, rushed, or heavy anymore.

Even though I didn't really understand "energy" or "Light" very well, I realized that there was something quite special, real, and tangible about the healing modalities, classes, activations and initiations from the Modern Mystery School that I was curious to learn more. I pursued further teaching and initiations, and it wasn't until I became a Ritual Master Novice (2011) that I realized there is a much bigger picture for humanity, and that I have a responsibility to me, my family, and community to become the best version of myself. I guess you could say that this understanding was the missing piece of the puzzle for that empty feeling I could never figure out.

During this time my mother, who also began this spiritual path of progression, encouraged me to pursue the Ancestral Clearing (2013). We learned about the negative influences in our family line, and had them removed. At that moment, it felt like every cell in my body had been released from the chains and bondage that had been holding me hostage for my whole life, that I hadn't even know were there. This was a pivotal moment in my struggle with depression! Since this was an ancestral clearing, unbeknownst to them, I noticed many other immediate and extended family members had also experience phenomenal positive benefits and changes.

By including spirituality into my life and understanding how the universe works, I have now created a phenomenal life for myself and family. When I look back I realized that since my Empower Thyself Initiation I noticed my choices and decisions have been much more personally supportive. I've changed what I spend my time and money on, and regularly invest in my self-care because I recognize my value now. Ultimately, I have been able to transform and transmute my life into one of freedom and joy. One of the teachings in the Universal Hermetic Ray Kabbalah Ascension Program is to become the "captain of your ship", which I have finally done. I have created an amazing kingdom for myself with beautiful house that I love coming home to, financial security, peace of mind, freedom, full choice of how I fill my schedule, and so much more. Most importantly I am able to share all of this with those who also want a high-quality life, and that is what eliminated that empty feeling. Many people say we're "lucky," but the only thing you could call luck was that I took the leap-of-faith and received a Life Activation all those years ago.

Stephanie's Story: Distance Healing Immediately Addresses Sexual Trauma
By Casey O'Connell

I had known Stephanie for quite a few years through my virtual contracting gig with a tech company based in California. A single mom age 52 living in California, she was firstly an incredible coach who supported our client base but also someone who I felt super comfortable going to whenever I needed just a little bit of personal support.

Stephanie had expressed interest in Energy Clearing work before and I'd referred her to a colleague nearer to her, but that never panned out. Months went by and I was going through something tough on my end, and reached out to her to set up a coaching session to talk through some of what was coming up. I really just needed someone to talk to and she had always been such a person! Since she had also continued to express her desire to receive some energy clearing, I figured it was a perfect opportunity to see if she wanted to trade her time for mine and receive a distance session from me.

Since we do not offer any distance energy clearing sessions within the Modern Mystery School, I mentioned that a Spark of Life Distance Healing might be a wonderful place to start. She gladly accepted, with zero expectation around what the session would accomplish, and we set up a date. The morning of her session, I texted Stephanie and told her that I was about to begin when she told me that she'd be a few minutes late, because her pup needed to use the bathroom! (These are the unexpected perks of distance sessions - they can be a bit flexible!) I could feel her excitement and anticipation building as I prepared for her session.

Now what's most interesting here is that I typically provide Spark of Life Distance Healing to clients for a specific purpose (i.e. cancer, Covid, back pain) yet this session was a totally open field! I did my thing and texted her directly afterwards to check in as I typically do with this type of healing since I'm not there with the person in the physical. She replied almost immediately with the feedback that she was blown away.

Unexpectedly, she felt the light and energy from the healing go directly to the parts of her field where she had been carrying deep, sexual trauma from childhood. She had spent decades utilizing all different types of methods to address it (therapy, EMDR, anxiety medication) and it had not budged until this healing. Nothing that she'd tried had even touched it, and as the practitioner, without me knowing one thing about her prior situation, the healing was able to address her deep-seated trauma in just one session. The following day she reached back out saying that it was as though she'd taken a happy pill! And that she'd be booking another one of these sessions in a month.

I continue to check in with her between sessions, and she continues to feel uplifted, clearer and more filled with hope and possibility.

There is truly nothing in the world like the feeling that comes as a healer within the Modern Mystery School Lineage when you genuinely cannot explain to your own client what has happened with anything other than: This truly is magick!

Nancy's Story: ADHD Disappeared After a Series of Sessions (Life Activation, Full Spirit Activation, Clearings, and more)
By Karla Clark

We all know people with ADHD. It can be so frustrating for the person with ADHD and also for the loved ones. Many people with ADHD get put in certain educational programs to try and help them, but sometimes those programs can make them feel more isolated and do not really help the social aspect of the person's life.

I had a client who was originally sent to me for a spell removal and aura clearing – this includes a cord cutting to remove old energies and attachments. This client – Nancy- had been through a series of toxic relationships and had just gotten out of a particularly bad one. Her friend had seen me for a clearing and Life Activation and knew that this work would help her and told her to come see me. She worked in the creative arts and was in her late 20s. She had rocky relationships with people she called her friends but who often did not seem to treat her like a good friend.

Nancy also had deep psychological harm and family trauma – addiction in the family, toxic and bullying sibling relationships, and a toxic environment at school growing up. She had been put in Special Ed because the teachers thought she had really severe ADHD, but she experienced emotional abuse and stifling in the classes.

After the Spell Removal and Aura Clearing session, she felt lighter and like she could feel her own boundaries. She liked that she did not feel so much of the energy of her family smothering her. She was in a really dire situation in her life, but the feeling she had after the session gave her a boost to help her begin to shift her life. She was looking forward to making a change.

She let me know that she had suffered from ADHD and mood issues for most of her life, and so we decided her next session would be the Life Activation – I know personally that it can help heal mood energies and the energies of the brain.

After her Life Activation, she felt more grounded and able to make decisions for herself. She did not feel like she wanted cigarettes anymore and was able to quit. She had been using cigarettes as an emotional crutch for many years. She was really happy to be done with cigarettes. Part of what was revealed to her through the process was that she also had complex PTSD from her childhood, and she was able to work on it and move through it and enter the most successful phase of her life.

Nancy also felt like she did not need her ADHD medication anymore, so she worked with her doctor to wean herself off and has not taken any of those medications for the last ten years (and she has actually been productive and made huge progress, working her life purpose as an artist!).

We worked together for a whole year, with Full Spirit Activation after the Life Activation. She said she felt like her life opened up after the Full Spirit Activation, and she was able to let people go from her life who were not healthy for her, including interacting and talking with some family members who were abusive or toxic to her.

After the Isis Healing she noticed that her emotions felt more manageable, and she felt the burnout she had been experiencing melting away. She was able to purge a huge backlog of old emotion, freeing her to be more "in the now" and in the driver's seat of her life.

At the end of a year of working together, she decided to step forward for the Empower Thyself Initiation. Initiation really changed her life. She was able to completely let go of old patterns and move into a whole new way of being – including producing her own art shows, which is part of her purpose and expression. She felt so free and was able to reformulate how she worked and did her business. She even went on a speaking circuit, educating professionals about mental health (in a fun, entertaining way).

Nancy really bloomed and shifted and began to express her true self, feel connected to her purpose, and she has been living her life purpose. She was so happy to be freed from the old patterns and the misery that had permeated her life until she found these tools. She is living proof that toxic family patterns and ADHD can be left behind.

Two: Physical Healing

"Do not be afraid of your difficulties. Do not wish you could be in other circumstances than you are. For when you have made the best of an adversity, it becomes the stepping stone to a splendid opportunity."

— H.P. Blavatsky

Christine's Story: Skeptical Scientist Healed of Two Debilitating Illnesses
By Christine Estrema

Growing up I was raised religious, but as a teenager I grew disillusioned with anything relating to spirituality or religion. My Mom joined a cult when I was about thirteen years old. When I was about sixteen, I started to question why we were a part of this organization. When I confronted my mother about why, she said that her husband (my step-father) would not have married her if she wasn't a part of the cult. That answer shocked me! I didn't believe this was a good enough reason to comply with what the cult was trying to teach us. So, at the age of sixteen, I left the cult and started to deprogram myself. I lived by sleeping at my friends' houses until I turned eighteen.

I went seeking for what I felt I could believe in. That turned out to be science. My love for the scientific method and research drew me in. I loved finding out new things about the world we lived in. I fell in love with science, and was really good at it. I got my Master's Degree in Cardiovascular Sciences. I worked for 15 years as a professional research scientist in the fields of cardiology and immune-oncology.

There are some taboo topics in the scientific community, and spirituality is one of them. I got so enamored by this process of proving and measuring things that I started rejecting anything that couldn't be "proven" this way. This, along with my upbringing in the cult, made me extremely skeptical of anything spiritual.

That started to change after a few years of battling two serious physical illnesses. I was so ill that I had to go on disability and barely had enough energy to leave the house. I tried so many remedies that didn't work. The years of illness with no solutions left me desperate, and finally open to trying almost anything.

The first illness began after falling down a hill in 2012. It triggered a condition called complex regional pain syndrome. My knee was in a lot of pain, and my leg from the knee down went numb and became blue from lack of circulation, with the pain spreading up the right side of my body. I started out with physical therapy and pain medication. The doctors ran and a lot of MRIs and various tests, but they didn't know what was causing my condition at first. I was undiagnosed for a couple years. The doctors told me they didn't know what caused it and there was nothing that they could fix. The pain got worse and worse over time. Eventually I ended up on opiates and getting steroid epidurals twice a year. The doctors recommended that I quit my job and go on disability, but I was stubborn, so I didn't at that time.

Since my doctors didn't have any real solutions, I started looking for alternative treatments, in holistic medicine, hypnosis, and shamanism. I noticed when I tried these methods I would feel better for a little while, but the overall trend was that I was getting worse. So it wasn't really working.

In 2016, I was working in a lab doing immune-oncology research. Someone who was not trained properly brought a sample of an experimental variation of Epstein-Barr virus into the lab and used it outside of containment. I got infected with the virus.

I got hit really hard with the virus. My viral load count was extremely high. I could barely get out of bed. The virus attacked my pericardium (the lining around the heart). With this condition, if you exert yourself too much, you could cause yourself to have a heart attack. So I was mostly bed-ridden. I would sleep most of the day. I set an alarm on my phone to remind me to wake up and drink water. I couldn't drive. Just getting from my bedroom upstairs to the front door downstairs was enough to wipe me out for the day.

The doctors said there was nothing they can do. Epstein Barr is not currently treatable. So that forced me to go on disability. I was in bed for about a year and a half. I was at the doctor's office several times a week. I couldn't drive myself because I would fall asleep. I would be picked up by a medical bus or Lyft. I had just bought my first house, but I couldn't enjoy it because I slept constantly.

On a good day, I would drag myself to sit in the sun outside in the back yard. But that was about all the energy I could muster. My life was bleak. I was having frequent panic attacks at any type of anxiety. I was constantly in pain, and by this point the pain had spread up to my entire right side of the body. With Epstein Barr syndrome they recommend you work your way up to exercise, but because I still had complex regional pain syndrome, I wasn't able to exercise without extreme pain.

Then one (rare) day I had enough energy to go out and do something. I looked online and found a meditation that was five minutes from my house. I took a Lyft there, and it ended up being hosted by The Modern Mystery School. At the meditation I learned about the Life Activation. I was just desperate at this point. Though I was very skeptical that God existed because I saw no evidence of it, a part of me knew I just wanted the Life Activation. Something inside of me just lit up when I heard about it. Every part of me wanted it, and I had no logical reason why. I thought, "Nothing the doctors have done has worked. I've tried everything else. I have nothing to lose. Why not?" I ended up receiving the Life Activation the next day.

Two days after my Life Activation, I drove to the grocery store and bought groceries for the first time in a year and a half. It was the first time I had enough energy to do this! I was really grateful to have that much energy. I felt conflicted. The first thing I did in my mind was go to, "this is a coincidence. Maybe right now is just the time I started to get better." But then I had a doctor's appointment a few days later, and they did blood work. It showed my viral load had dropped significantly, and it had been up for the past year and a half.

Yet, I wasn't completely convinced yet. I had a conflict in my mind. I felt better, but I also thought, "This is a coincidence. Correlation does not equal causation." But then I went back to receive additional sessions, such as the Full Spirit Activation and Etheric Reconstruction sessions. Every time I had a session, I always had a dramatic shift. Sometimes it was health related, but sometimes it was emotional. What kept me going back was that every time I had a session I improved and kept getting better over time. With everything else I'd tried, I would get worse over time. The chronic pain was also improving.

Then my (future) Guide suggested I go to Empower Thyself Initiation. I didn't really know what to expect, but everything else she did was working, so I went. Even after, I had a hard time accepting that these tools with no scientific evidence were working. It went against the training I'd received. It went against the culture of science that I'd been in. It was a mental struggle where I was torn inside.

This struggle drove me to go to Healer's Academy in 2018. This is where they teach you how to do the Life Activation for others. When I arrived, I told one of the instructors who is a medical doctor that I was there to prove it was all bullshit. She got a real kick out of that! She laughed and said, "Good luck with that!"

During Healer's Academy, I felt things I didn't expect to feel. And I felt them before the instructors told us about them. If I'd felt them after they told us, I would have thought it was mental conditioning, but it happened before. For example, they asked us to scan the client in a specific area, and I felt very clearly there was something that needed to be removed. Then they taught us how to remove the block I had already felt was there! And after I completed the process, I could feel that the block was no longer there. This type of thing happened several times during the training. So finally, I allowed myself to just accept that maybe this is valid and to just allow myself to receive and experience the training.

I got home from Healer's Academy and decided to start my own "experiments." I started Life Activating people not because I fully believed it worked, but to see what happened. What I found in almost all cases was that people's lives visibly improved. The most consistent and significant thing I heard was that people's stress levels were reduced. I also saw people break addictions. I saw people increase in abundance.

After seeing the results from my clients, I started to believe there was something real to this even though I couldn't fully explain it. And I was starting to get better myself. These two things together allowed me to accept that something was actually happening. I believed enough that I went to the next step of initiation, called Ritual Master 1.0. Since that initiation, I've never had to see my doctors again for the conditions that had completely altered my life. My chronic pain was completely gone immediately after the initiation! I walked out and my leg wasn't blue anymore. My doctor saw me the next week because I had an injection scheduled. When she saw me, she freaked out! She pulled in another doctor to examine me. Both of them said my immediate recovery wasn't possible! They took photos to document it and said it was like I'd never been sick! Please see the end of this story for the photo evidence.

I should also mention that during the time I was suffering from these chronic conditions, I was under the care of a psychologist. When I started taking classes with The Modern Mystery School, I had some reservations because of my experience growing up in a cult. So I was on high alert for any signals that this might be a cult. So when I went to Empower Thyself Initiation, Healer's Academy, did Universal Hermetic Ray Kabbalah, and until I did Ritual Master, I would share my experiences with the psychologist to get her perspective. She would ask me questions and we would work through it. She said, "You're getting better. I'm going to advise you to continue. If something weird happens, let me know. But everything I'm seeing so far is good."

My psychologist's advice gave me enough confidence to continue pursuing the classes and the healings. But I was still on high alert. I even told my Guide, "I have my running shoes on." After I completed Ritual Master 1.0, I started to reflect on the difference the school made in my life and my interactions with my Guide. My Guide never once told me what to do, which would have been a huge red flag for me. And she spoke very honestly, very pure. I could feel her sincerity. And that allowed me to trust a little bit.

When I reflected on the difference in made in my life, I saw that my health dramatically improved, my emotional state improved, I had no more pain, my PTSD went away. I was enjoying life more than I ever had. Even in the bad moments, life felt like an adventure, whereas before it would have sent me into a panic attack. I had energy again. I was also falling in love with the teachings of the school. Unlike in university you study it with your mind, the stuff I was learning with the Mystery School unfolded over time and I found myself understanding the world and the universe differently, and even science differently. It was the missing piece I was looking for that is completely energetic, and beyond the mental level.

My life today is really awesome. It's vibrant. It feels like I'm really alive. I'm discovering every day more and more about who I am and my capabilities. In science I was searching for this hidden world that I didn't know I was looking for, but I didn't receive the energies to experience it until I found this school. The biggest shift I've had is what it really means to love myself. Sometimes loving yourself isn't easy; it's actually doing the hardest thing. But when we love ourselves and fill our cups, we have more joy. And it creates a stable foundation where the world can throw whatever at us, but we're still at peace.

I'll give an example of how I love myself so much more now. I wrote a list of the things I wanted in a relationship. And then I realized those were actually the qualities of what I wanted from myself. So I started giving those things to myself. And it took so much pressure off the people around me because I wasn't expecting those things from my relationships. It's given me a lot of room and space to go through my own process of growth because I'm not expecting people to provide those for me.

My life still includes science. I do part-time consulting for bio-tech companies. And I am also working on a confidential project with algae. What I can say is that I'm using some of the tools from The Modern Mystery School to see if I can affect the growth rate of the algae. I'm also a Guide with The Modern Mystery School. I attract a lot of clients in nursing. They say that I provide something to them that they've been searching for and couldn't find before. My nursing clients come to me and they're very stressed. After the Life Activation their careers tend to shift. For example, two of my clients switched careers to become traveling nurses, which they report to be more fun, less stressful and pays more.

In my personal relationships, I've found that I'm getting continually better at setting healthy boundaries and also making heart connections. I used to be stuck in the mental state. I also have a really big community of people in the Mystery School around me, and it's really great to have this. I found in my communication with people when problems arise, it's smoother. I'm able to admit when I made a mistake and accept others' mistakes and move forward more quickly. This is new for me. In the science world you were expected to not make mistakes and not be seen in a bad light. Letting go of those false expectations of perfection has made my life more authentic and it's so much easier to have fulfilling relationships.

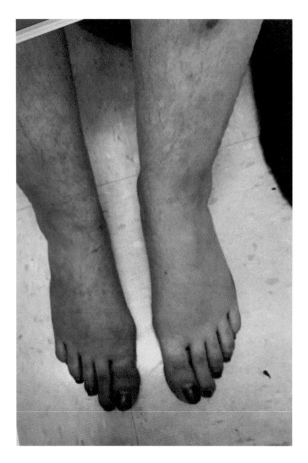 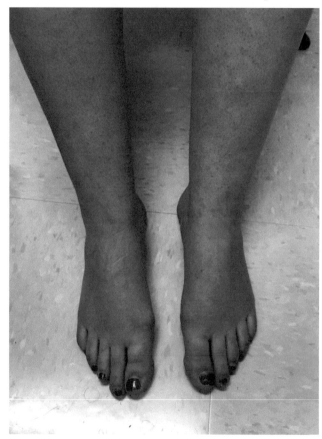

Christine's leg before her Ritual

Master 1.0 initiation

Christine's one week after her

Ritual Master 1.0 initiation

Ronald's Story: Speedy Covid Recovery from Ventilator to Outpatient
By Dawn Ressel

It was April 2020, in the very beginning of the Covid-19 pandemic. The hospitals were overwhelmed with patients and there was little known about how to treat this virus. Ronald was in his late sixties and was admitted to the hospital with Covid-19. He got very sick, very quickly.

Only a few days after symptoms started he was in the ICU. His health declined rapidly and they put him on a ventilator. Even this early in the pandemic it was clear that a person's chance of survival once they reached this point was not good. His doctors were not hopeful about Ronald's chances of survival as he continued to worsen.

One of Ronald's family members heard about distance healings from The Modern Mystery School and asked for help. Two days after Ronald got on the ventilator, he received a distance Ensofic Ray healing in the evening. The next morning, he received a distance Spark of Life session.

Within 24 hours, Ronald's vital signs started to improve dramatically. He was also conscious and aware and was able to stay awake much longer. He was taken off the ventilator. After two days Ronald's health improved so dramatically that he was released from the hospital to go home and finish his recovery. The doctors and nurses were stunned by his rapid recovery and had no real explanation for it.

After he returned home, Ronald was interviewed by his local new station. They heard of his miraculous recovery and wanted to share the story to give people hope. His recovery at home was steady, and within weeks he was feeling much better and able to walk around fairly normally. Ronald was on the brink of death, but after two distance healing sessions he rebounded to an almost full recovery within weeks. Ronald is quite happy now. He recently got married to the woman he had been in a relationship with since before he got ill with Covid.

Ronald's story is a dramatic one, but not the only one. There are many other people with Covid-19 who received these distance healings who ranged moderate to severe symptoms and healed much faster than expected as a result. In tandem with the appropriate level of traditional medical approaches, these distance healings have helped people across the world recover from Covid-19 much faster.

Andrea's Story: Healing Long-Standing Anemia with the Bloodline Session
By Karla Clark

A wonderful and creative woman named Andrea (in her 30s) came to me in 2011 in Seattle because she had extreme anemia that was affecting her life. We knew each other because our young children were friends. She had even referred people to me for healing and initiation without ever having come to see me herself for healing before. She considered herself to be an atheist, but she was willing to try anything. She was really suffering. She usually enjoyed creating art and working on community projects and events. The anemia had been going on a while – leaving her tired, pale, dizzy, prone to headaches, and feeling cold all the time.

Anemia is often caused by heavy periods for many women. It can also have other causes. Some women cannot use birth control pills or IUDs to help stop the blood loss. There are estimates that 3 million to 8 million women per year experience anemia in the United States.

Andrea had been under care of a medical doctor. For anemia often doctors often tell patients to eat more red meat and to increase iron and Vitamin B and C intake. She had tried that advice and supplements for many months with no results or change. Her hemoglobin was extremely low, and she was even taking iron IV infusions, which can actually be quite dangerous. Her blood cell counts were not responding. She was exhausted, stressed, just really wanting to feel better, to be able to do normal activities, and feel like she was being a good mom.

I was happy to help. I had also gone through very similar symptoms- really wretched anemia that did not respond to normal treatment. I had tried extreme dietary measures, acupuncture, and herbs. I was left extremely physically and mentally exhausted as well as frustrated with my body. The thing that finally helped me was providing Bloodline Sessions to others as well as receiving them.

Andrea wanted to have energy to play with her kids, be a happy wife, create, and dance. After one Bloodline Session, she felt more energetic and had hope.

After her 2nd Bloodline Session (about 1 month after the first) she started to finally absorb the iron in the IVs. Her doctor was happy to see that her body was beginning to respond to treatment.

After her 3rd session, her blood cells began to increase. She was joyful – she felt like she had more energy and she was so glad that something was finally working!

She was able to recover fully about 6 months after her 1st session, when prior to receiving the Bloodline Session no treatments were helping. I had the experience personally of trying natural and medical remedies with no improvement for nearly a year, and then within three months of working with the Bloodline Session, my blood cells began to rise.

I have experienced it myself – from being exhausted and hopeless - not knowing what to do - and then having the hope and the improvement of Bloodline Session.

Andrea was so happy to recover. Now - more than ten years later - she still thanks me for the help.

Kevin's Story: Long-Haul Covid with Parosmia Reversed with Ensofic Ray
By Karla Clark

Kevin, a father and husband in his 40s, who had been ill with long haul Covid – to the point where he had no hope and did not know if he would ever enjoy life again – came in to see me for Ensofic Ray Healing. This is the story of his miraculous recovery. He now lives a life of joy once more!

Before having Covid, Kevin was a vibrant person – living life with fun and joy with his family, and also enjoying exercise and staying fit. Life was very good!

In December of 2020, Kevin became very ill with Covid. He had breathing issues, heart palpitations, extreme fatigue, pain, and even mood issues. One of the symptoms that badly bothered him was parosmia – he not only could not smell the normal scent of an object – for example lettuce, or an orange – it was worse than smelling nothing. He smelled off-putting and disturbing smells like sewer, rotting meat, and strange chemical smells. Imagine if lettuce smelled like chemicals and sewer! There were only two foods that were not entirely repulsive to him – one kind of tortilla and one kind of protein powder. Everything else smelled nauseating and repellant.

He had been working with physicians and had tried acupuncture and other modalities as possible treatments. Unfortunately, nothing was helping. He was not sleeping, his mood was very low, and he could not enjoy his normal activities or feel like he was really connecting with his family. He could not exercise. He was losing hope.

In August of 2021, his wife reached out to me – she knew that I was an energy healer and had heard some of my stories of miraculous results. They were ready to try anything! I set up time for Kevin to come in for his first session and really hoped that it would help – I had not worked on anyone with long haul Covid in person up to that point. I had only worked on critically ill folks using distance healing.

After his 1st appointment August 14, 2020, he had more energy and started to feel more positive. The next day he was able to smell food and noticed that it smelled good! That is after one session, and it gave him hope.

After his 2nd appointment August 21, Kevin really seemed to be doing better- he said he had more energy, felt more positive, and went to the gym (!!!) as well as getting some good sleep! He also said that things weren't smelling bad - he still has loss of regular scent, but now he was not smelling "bad stuff," which was a big win! His chest pain abated and he could breathe down into his lungs towards his abdomen – this was a great improvement!

After his 3rd appointment (August 28) – I received a note from his wife:

"I am absolutely seeing progressive improvement with him. I would love for him to keep seeing you. The fact that his chest pain and breathing issue has pretty much fully subsided - after nine months of struggling to gain breath- is absolutely incredible. He's definitely recognizing more smells and told me this morning he's gonna start doing 2 days at the gym which tells me his energy level is definitely improving. I couldn't be happier to see progress with him and of course we will continue to do whatever it takes to keep him in a positive mindset and having more and more victories. I appreciate you more than you know and so glad we connected to do this treatment for him. ♡"

I was overjoyed to receive the note, and so happy for him and his improvement in life! In order to sustain the improvements, I ended the series with a Life Activation – a session that helps with the energy for mental clarity and also helps reawaken the senses, which I thought could potentially help with healing the energy for the sense of smell. I also find that Life Activation can help us maintain the energy of other healings that we receive (for me I even hold my chiropractic adjustments longer than a usual client – I think because of my Life Activation)!

I was so excited for him about his progress, I asked if I could create a case summary in order to approach university research long-haul programs. There are studies being performed to support folks with long haul Covid symptoms. Currently there are at least 6000 people in the San Diego Area with long haul Covid and about 1200 with parosmia. Some clinicians are offering nerve cauterization for that symptom, which is permanent.

I hope to be able to do a clinical trial of Ensofic Ray Healing for folks with parosmia, to give hope and healing to other sufferers. Now, almost a year later, Kevin is living the life he loves, having fun with his family and staying healthy and exercising.

Susan's Story: Painful Dermatitis and Psoriasis Healed through Ensofic Ray
By Dr. Kate Bartram Brown

I have been teaching and sharing sessions in the lineage of King Salomon for over 12 years now. As a doctor of Natural Medicine and the owner of a global business I have dedicated my life to finding methods to support my health and my business.

After many years of searching, trial, and error, I 'stumbled' upon the Modern Mystery School. What happened after that day and each day since I can only call Magick. Something that works outside of logic.

My own story, like many others is one of constant miracles. Upon being asked to share a story in the hope of inspiring you, the reader, I wanted to make sure that I chose a journey that would help even the most skeptical mind, to stop and consider that perhaps, just perhaps there is another way of well-being. And that indeed life is full of magick.

I met Susan through her sister, a good friend of mine. She had suffered so much over the years with a skin condition that was extremely painful, so much so that her doctors had placed her on several drugs. Her skin condition was diagnosed as Seborrheic Dermatitis plus Psoriasis. She was originally given an antibiotic with no results. It was then followed by:

- Clobetasol Prop Solutions (which had burned her).

- She had 3 bottles of Methylprednisolone (or what we would know as Steroid pills). Ketoconazole Cream.

- Triamcinolone Betamethasone. She had tried 4 different prescriptions over 18 months and nothing had worked.

In addition to the above Susan has used coconut oil and olive oil.

Susan was looking for an option to stop the discomfort. She no longer wanted to be on medication for this skin issue when it wasn't helping it.

Angela's skin was so sore, I wanted to help, so I suggested Ensofic Ray. The 3-session protocol must be done 7 days apart. I was in Kentucky for that period of time so it all fell into place perfectly.

I asked Susan if I could take a photo and perhaps document any changes in her skin. It was all over her body. I took photos of her face and her legs. The patches of the skin that were affected were red, raised from her skin with dry areas. I can't imagine how awful it must have been for her.

I explained to Susan that I could not guarantee the outcome, but I had previously seen miracles, with my own eyes, using this very same protocol. One such miracle was a lady spoke after nine months of being unable to speak due to a stroke.

I knew that the Ensofic Ray 3 session Protocol would work but I was unsure how that would look and how quickly it would work.

To give you some background The Ensofic Ray is the highest, brightest, and most powerful ray of energy. It has the qualities of purity, clarity, and focused concentration. This ray has the power to clear and heal negative thoughts and patterns. It is the 1st ray of creation; it is pure, straight to the point and penetrates right to the core to activate the codes of divinity within you

In this modality the breath of God is used to awaken the 'I am' presence within you helping you feel more connected to the oneness of all that is.

This healing modality is a process of re-orienting body, soul, and spirit to each other for absolute alignment: first, by destroying imbalanced physical, mental, and emotional patterns that prevent our highest potential; second, by sealing our physical vessels (our bodies) to contain this highest vibration; and third, by harmonizing our structures (mental, emotional, and physical) so that we can create a full LIFE resolved of conflict.

This is a great modality for those lacking passion for life, lacking desire, feeling like they are off track from their potential and purpose, or stuck in a rut. It awakens the desire to love and manifest that limitless light here in the physical. Space is very specially prepared. A virtual temple is created as the world of spirit is called in.

The Ensofic Ray series also:

- Heightens vibration of the body, allowing you to release lower energies that cause illness
- Realigns your physical body and soul with your purpose and potential
- Increases consciousness of spiritual energies helping you to connect to your divine potential
- Restores internal unity and heals the rift of separation both within and without
- Gently and powerfully releases old wounds and suffering held within your being
- Assists you in managing your life with clarity, wisdom, and grace

This healing modality covers so much, and goes so deep but I was too intrigued to see what would happen in Susan's situation. This was a first time for me with this ailment.

After the first session Susan went home and I didn't see her for 7 days. When she came back to see me for the second session, I was blown away. Already there were visible results. Please see the end of this story for the photo evidence.

After the 3rd session the skin complaint had almost but disappeared! She was over the moon. I took photos as results were clear to see with the naked eye, it was truly a miracle. Susan wanted everyone to know.

We didn't know how long this would last, or whether we would need to top up in some way. We carried on documenting the 'experiment'.

Why did I choose this story? Well, this 3-session protocol is only available in the Lineage and shared by 2nd step initiates. Here is where the magick can be found. The path of initiation is the most powerful path on the planet. How can I best share that other than through my own experience or photo evidence?! It's quite rare to be able to capture healing visually, and we did just that.

Any skin issue, disease, or mental health issue is a result of the unhealed parts of us. Creams and tablets will help with the symptoms ... well sometimes, but the issues will pop up elsewhere or not go away. Yet when we undertake deep healing in our emotional, spiritual, mental, soul, body and take a whole-being approach to well-being this is when we start to see the real healing take place. This is what happened in Susan's case. What happened next?

Susan took the class Empower Thyself, was initiated, and was able to manage her own healing from here on and has not seen a flare up since.

Sometimes we need that helping hand to kick-start the healing. In the Modern Mystery School we give you the tools to support yourself, and that is why we see longer lasting results in all areas of wellbeing.

It has now been over four years since we first took these photos. We will continue to document any changes.

If you wish to find out more, I would be very happy to chat and share different healing and progression options for your whole wellbeing and success.

www.modernmsyteryschooluk.com

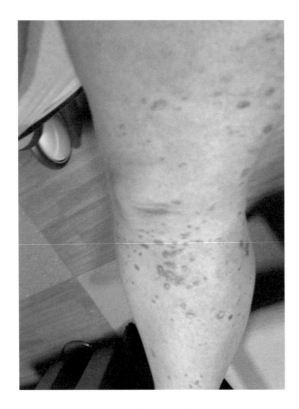 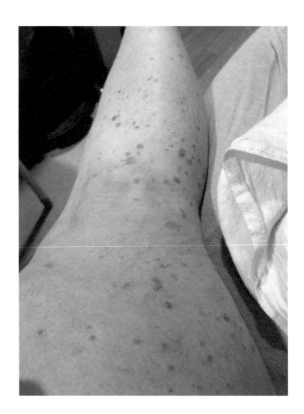

Susan's leg before Ensofic Ray Treatments *Susan's other leg before Ensofic Ray Treatments*

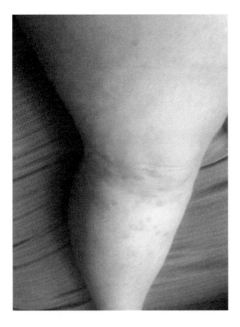

Susan's leg after three Ensofic Ray Treatments

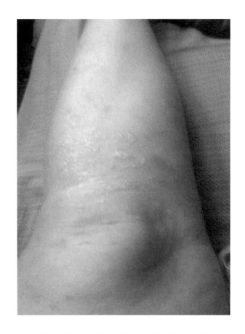

Susan's other leg after Ensofic Ray Treatments

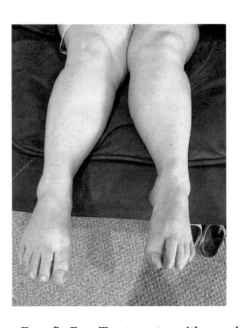

Susan's legs 6 years after her Ensofic Ray Treatments, with no additional treatments needed

Three: Self Love

"Your sacred space is where you can find yourself over and over again."

— Joseph Campbell

Dawn's Story: Overcoming Co-Dependency
By Dawn Ressel

In 2016, Independence Day took on a whole new, very personal meaning for me. It became about my own independence. In late 2015 I asked my ex-husband Ted for a divorce. It was the hardest thing I'd ever done. It was the first time I made a really difficult choice to listen to my heart and soul and trust the divine, regardless of the consequences. There was fallout for sure. But when I look back, there is no question I did the right thing.

When I met Ted, I was afraid of everything. My generalized anxiety disorder kept me in a state of near constant fear. He came into my life and he was kind and adoring. He was funny and extremely intelligent. I never felt bored being around him. He did things for me that I was afraid to do, like driving. And for him, I did the things he didn't want to do, like holding down a steady job. We created a safe feeling, co-dependent relationship.

The problem was the foundation of our marriage was our weaknesses. We had a great friendship that could have existed very well on its own. But as a marriage, it could only work as long as neither of us changed. That's how co-dependence operates, based on the agreement that we don't outgrow the things that keep us dependent.

I truly believe Ted did the very best he could with the tools and capacity he had at that time. And he really deeply loved me in the best way he knew how. But I needed something radically different. I needed to learn how to be on my own.

After I asked for the divorce, Ted was very angry with me, and I understood why. When he expressed his anger, I did my best to stay neutral and not let it affect me, and I mostly succeeded.

Until one day in March of 2016, after our divorce paperwork was filed but not yet finalized, he sent me an email. He said that I was horrible, selfish, cruel, and so on.

It hurt deeply. It made me question myself and wonder if what he said was true. I started sobbing uncontrollably. I was just at the beginning of my spiritual journey, but in that moment all I could do was reach for the divine. I prayed. I pleaded with the universe to give me a sign. Please, please give me a sign that I am doing the right thing. I prayed and sobbed for what must have been half an hour, just reiterating again and again. Please give me a sign if I'm doing the right thing.

I got my sign so quickly that it's almost unfathomable. Later that same day, I went to my mailbox. There was a large manila envelope from the Court of San Diego County. Inside was the response from the divorce court. It said the judge had approved the divorce request. And that our divorce would be finalized on JULY 4, 2016. Independence Day!

From that moment on, I firmly believed in my decision. Even Ted remarked on the significance of the date and started to see things differently. He forgave me and even told me that he understood why I did what I did. We became friends again, both of us on a new foundation.

Three years after Ted and I got divorced, he passed away. The last seven years of our marriage he was terminally ill with kidney disease. That's what made it so difficult for me to ask for a divorce. I stayed in the marriage much longer than I might have otherwise, partly out of guilt, partly out of fear of the unknown, and partly out of fear of judgment.

I worried what other people might think. Unfortunately, there is often a stigma that comes with divorce, and in my case, I was harshly judged by some for leaving a sick husband. But the more I got in touch with my own soul, the less I cared what others thought about my life choices.

Living an inauthentic life like the one I was living shreds the soul. By the end, I was in our marriage simply out of obligation. Though I cared deeply for Ted, I never really loved him as I believe a person should love their husband. From the beginning, the marriage was a safety net. And once I started to heal myself, the marriage felt like a burden. There was no joy in it.

Part of my healing journey has been to forgive myself for divorcing Ted. His condition had no hope of recovery. However, I was his emotional support system. When I look back, I see that even though he would have never chosen it, the divorce also helped him claim some of his own independence. He moved back to be closer to his family, which allowed him to spend the last years of his life close to his mother and siblings who had been on the other side of the country for most of his illness. He reunited with old friends. He no longer relied solely on me.

Since my divorce, I've been on an epic journey to reclaim my independence. You see July 04, 2016 was the very first step in the journey, not in any way the end. I had so much healing to do in order to get from a woman who was just barely out of a long-term co-dependent marriage to a woman who is truly independent. I can really only say within the few months or so that I am finally living as an independent, sovereign being. It's taken six years of hard work to get here. Healing, undoing, learning, rebuilding, reclaiming.

The number one thing that's helped me claim my independence is Universal Hermetic Ray Kabbalah. In Kabbalah we learn about living life in balance: what we call the middle pillar. Independence lives on the middle pillar. On one end of the imbalance is attachment. On the other end is avoidance and fear of commitment. And in the middle is independence and sovereignty.

In these past six years I've fumbled my way through dating, trying to have a healthy romantic relationship in my life. I've had some good experiences. And I've also made many mistakes. But each encounter taught me lessons. I got to see parts of myself that were hidden, unhealed and in the shadows. In the structure of a co-dependent relationship I never had to address these shadows. But in the reflection of a new romantic interest, there was nowhere to hide.

During my first Kabbalah tree in 2019 I started dating a man who was not emotionally available. I settled for less than I deserved because I was lonely and found him very attractive. But he couldn't meet me where I was. The very night after my Kabbalah final ascension I contacted him. I told him I wouldn't see him anymore. I simply couldn't tolerate settling for that in my new life. I was on a new level of self-love, a higher vibration.

In my most recent Kabbalah tree that ended in June 2022, I set a goal to find my divine partner. I naively thought, I've done so much work on myself. Surely I'll receive him now. Maybe he'll even show up on my doorstep with a big bow on top! I look back on that notion now and laugh. I had no idea what I was really asking for. I got what I was ready for, but not what I imagined.

It reminds me of a scene from the movie *Evan Almighty*, where Morgan Freeman plays the character of God and states, "Let me ask you something. If someone prays for patience, you think God gives them patience? Or does he give them the opportunity to be patient? If he prayed for courage, does God give him courage, or does he give him opportunities to be courageous? If someone prayed for the family to be closer, do you think God zaps them with warm fuzzy feelings, or does he give them opportunities to love each other?"

Well, instead of getting my life partner with a bow on top, I got some of the hardest lessons that I still had to learn in order to ready for such a relationship. I met a wonderful man who acted as my mirror for many months. In his reflection, I saw all the places where I had already healed and become worthy. I saw how far I had come in loving myself and being ready for love from another. But I also saw the shadows - where parts of me were still stuck in attachment and co-dependency. I saw where I still didn't trust God to support me or where I didn't trust myself to create the type of relationship that I truly desired in my heart.

During this process, I went through bitter heartbreak and disappointment. But I've found meaning in that suffering. It helped me identify and let go of parts of myself that were blocking my own light. They were the remnants keeping me from being truly independent.

One thing I learned through all of this is that a divine union has to be built on the foundation of two whole people, living in the middle pillar. They have to first be living in their power as sovereign beings in their own kingdom/queendom. They have to live independently without either the fear of being alone or the fear of commitment. They have to know their own worth and be ready to receive nothing less than what they are worthy of receiving. They enter the relationship because they truly want to give love to this other person, not because they want to receive back something they lack within themselves.

Two independent, whole beings working together on the same mission, on a foundation of love for each and themselves can create more than either of them alone. However, two unhealed people compensating for each other create less than a person alone striving to become whole. Because the two hold each other back. When I decided to divorce, I didn't reject him. I chose myself.

Am I ready yet for that relationship I've been asking God for? I can't say for sure. I guess I'll know when I know. But I am closer than I ever have been. And more importantly, I am at peace with the not knowing. That's new.

Since my last Kabbalah final ascension, I feel a sense of surrender and trust that I've never felt before. I don't feel afraid to be alone. I love myself. And I know that I deserve to be loved by someone else in the same way that I love myself. I no longer fret that I'm running out of time to find the right person. I believe there is a plan that is set to work out in divine timing.

Right here right now, I will only accept a relationship that honors who I truly am. I would rather be by myself than in the wrong relationship. I love myself so much that I won't accept anything less than a relationship that makes my already amazing life even better.

When I reflect back on the decision to get divorced, it was truly one of the hardest decisions of my life. But it was also the correct decision. The right thing to do is sometimes the hardest thing to do. It might have been easier to change nothing and keep going day by day, very sure of the outcome. But I would have accomplished nothing to help myself or to fulfill my own purpose.

It is our highest responsibility in this life to honor ourselves above all else and to love ourselves above everyone else. Sometimes that means others will be unhappy with our choices. Had I stayed married, I would not be where I am today: writing this book, having undergone this epic healing journey that I get to experience and tell others about, and having the privilege of helping others with their healing journey. I would be living a much lesser, fairly joyless life.

Our joy comes from fulfilling our purpose. And the ultimate goal of this life is to experience joy. Perhaps this story will prompt you to imagine a life of greater joy for yourself and take the steps to get there.

Denise's Story: The Most Important Relationship of All
By Jeannie Vassos

I knew Denise before I became a Life Activation Practitioner. She was in her mid-thirties, skilled in internet technology, administration, and marketing, had a cat, and was always trying to improve herself whether it be mentally, physically or emotionally. However, she was in a long-term relationship that she knew she wasn't truly happy with. After 12 years, the relationship still didn't feel authentic. She had an inkling that part of the problem was that she always put her partner and his family ahead of her and her own family. But she couldn't see any other way to behave differently because she didn't want to rock-the-boat. She loved her partner and thought they could grow closer with time, but felt like she was endlessly waiting for it to get better.

She didn't really know what a Life Activation was, but was intrigued that I was going for 5-day training to Healer's Academy to learn it and approached me shortly afterwards. She had the Life Activation (2011) and she said that during the session she felt like she was being pulled up to stand straighter, almost as though she became taller.

In the days following she noticed how her negative self-talk lessened. Surprisingly, she noticed she was not as addicted to her phone as she normally was, and that she didn't feel as guilty when she wasn't working. She mentioned how instead of constant worry and angst about working, she was able to actually take a break, enjoy being outside in nature, and think of something else for a while. This newfound calm enabled her to be more productive and creative with her work and her business as a holistic nutritionist increased.

A year later she said that she realized, while she was in the Life Activation session with me, that she needed to leave her partner. It took that year to solidify the decision and make concrete future plans before she moved into her own place. By then she was ready for the Empower Thyself Initiation (2012). She found that the transformation after the initiation and working with the rituals supported her greatly during the break-up and move. Time and time again she has explained the experience as getting back to herself again, being herself again, following her intuition, and making future choices that feel right and good.

Denise is also professionally trained singer, and after leaving her relationship she joined a local choir and began to sing on a regular basis again. She kept her dating life to a minimum because she didn't want to jump into anything without getting back to her true self, but her business blossomed by attracting more high-profile clients. Because she is able to work from anywhere, after a few years in Toronto she moved back to her university town where she had always felt most "at home", and she extended her business to include coaching. There, she met the love of her life (2014), moved in together, got engaged, and are now married. They've added another cat or two, and the house is very full when her husband's adult daughters come to visit.

By investing in herself, and honoring her goals, desires and recognizing her value, she is now in a loving marriage, has a successful business, and lives a purposeful life.

Barbara's Story: Healing from Depression, Heartbreak, and Reclaiming Her Power
By Phyllis Fran Livera

Barbara met the love of her life in high school. They have been friends for years. Nevertheless, she married another man and had a daughter with him. After five years of marriage, he told her he wanted a divorce; separated from her; and told her she needed to move out of the house, which was in his name.

She moved into her sister's home where she was able to live in a small attic which was set up as an apartment. During the separation her husband had visitation rights to see his daughter. Through her daughter, she discovered that her husband was living with a young woman and the woman was pregnant. This woman had a baby boy 2 months after Barbara moved out and they became engaged.

Her daughter told Barbara that when she spent weekends with her father he would leave her at his cousin's home to play with her children. Her father did not spend time with her, but spent more time with his fiancée and baby boy. She always returned home upset and sad.

Barbara felt very deceived, disrespected, and traumatized to discover how badly he treated his daughter during visitations.

Besides all this, her ex-husband was moving to England to continue his work with an international insurance firm. He wanted Barbara and her daughter to also move to England.

Since Barbara didn't want to move to England, she fought for custody of her daughter and began, what turned out to be, the biggest custody battle for her daughter's life.

By this time, Barbara had gained 65 pounds and had lost her 110 svelte figure. She was upset about her weight, which led her to binge eating and yo-yo dieting.

That's when she called me to assist her. When I met her she was depressed, disheveled, and unkempt. Through my spiritual intake process I suggested that the Life Activation would assist her in her healing process and her journey to heal herself. We set up our first appointment for the Life Activation session.

After the Life Activation session, I scheduled her 2 days later for Emotional Cord Cutting and Spell Removal. I was shocked when she returned for her second session. She was confident well dressed and wore perfume. It was the most amazing physical transformation I've seen.

We talked afterward, and she continued to see me on and off for meditations, full moon ceremonies and other events. Each time I met her, she may have been beset by challenges but after each session, she always was more successful in dealing with her ex-husband and his manipulative and exploitative behaviors.

She did get full custody of her daughter and moved out of the USA and married the love of her life. She is very happy and feels empowered after receiving the Life Activation and Full Spirit Activation.

Four: Relationships

"We are travelers on a cosmic journey, stardust, swirling and dancing in the eddies and whirlpools of infinity. Life is eternal. We have stopped for a moment to encounter each other, to meet, to love, to share. This is a precious moment. It is a little parenthesis in eternity."

— Paulo Coelho

Amber's Story: From Mr. Very Wrong to Mr. Very Right
By Amber Campbell

I was not sure how I was going to share my story. There are so many layers and different timelines. I thought about what the biggest shift in my life was from this path, and I came to realize it was hope.

When I was younger I suffered from anxiety and depression. As I got older I would still experience these from time to time, and I just thought that was part of the human experience.

In December 2014 I decided to go back to school to become a Holistic Nutritionist. I made the bold leap and moved to a big city to go to school full time. At this time life felt good. I was excited and ready for a new adventure.

I made friends with my roommates and quickly realized I needed to find a job. The typical stress of balancing work and school came in, but I was able to manage by making friends and still having fun.

In order to stay afloat I decided to start a second job and drop down to part-time school. This new job was super fun, and I got to spend my days outside.

I met a lot of really awesome people at this job and became quite close with a few. I also met my biggest lesson.

Billy started later in the season, and he was the loud somewhat obnoxious type. He liked to have fun and joke around. He showed interest in me and was very upfront about it. At the time I was interested in and sort of seeing someone else. Over the season Billy had seemed to make me his goal. I was not interested in anything more than friendship.

A group of guys from out of town ended up coming to work at our park doing maintenance. They came with their campers and trailers and lived onsite. Sometimes after work my friends and I would hang out with them. One night we had a party and I ended up hooking up with one of them. Billy found out and got very angry. He was upset that I would hook up with someone else when I knew he wanted to. He started spreading rumours about me.

It got to the point that I had to go to the police to see what could be done. The police recognized his name right away since he was already in their system because of other offenses. There was not much to be done other than having work not schedule us together.

During this time, I was also dealing with the recent loss of my grandma, my grandpa being diagnosed with Leukemia, and I myself, having to have a treatment to rid my body of pre-cancerous cells.

I started drinking and getting high during the day. This seemed to be the only thing that would ease the anxiety and depression I was feeling.

At the end of the season we had a staff outing. I knew Billy would be there, and I felt anxious the whole time. We had become friends over the season, and I was hurt that he would spread rumours about me and be so controlling. I wanted to make amends so I asked him to talk. I shared with him how I was upset with his behaviour and he apologized. He never meant it to go that far but he was hurt that I didn't want to date him. We made up and started our friendship again.

The work season had ended and I found another job. Billy and I started hanging out more since we did enjoy each other's company. A thing about Billy I should mention is that he had another friend Roxy. She wanted to date Billy but he wanted to be just friends with her. So, you can see I was in this weird love triangle. Roxy wanted Billy, Billy wanted me, and I wanted someone else.

Over time I decided we could try this open relationship thing. Billy would share his time between me and Roxy, and I was free to date whomever else I wanted to as well. This became complicated as you can imagine.

Since the work season had ended, Billy decided to go back to one of his old ventures: being a pimp. Roxy was all for it since she wanted to pay off school debt. This also meant they would be spending more time together. Billy had asked me to join him and shared how being blonde and pretty would give me an advantage and we could charge more. I was not into it.

One night I was hanging out with some girlfriends when Billy called me. He was out "working" with a new girl he met on Tinder. Part of me was jealous that he was hanging out with another girl and the other part could care less. I was very intoxicated and high when he called, and he said I could come hang out with him while she was working. My friends did not like Billy and suggested I stay. He could hear them in the background, which fuelled his anger. He came and picked me up with this new girl, Brenda. She drove my car back to his place since I couldn't. On the way back to his place his phone rang. It was a client. He told me to answer. The guy on the phone was talking in code that I did not understand. I ended up losing him a potential client.

When we got back to Billy's place, my ego took over. Looking at Brenda, I rethought Billy's offer of working with him. I thought, "I'm prettier than her, and if she can do this, then so can I." I ended up going back to the hotel with them. Billy took pictures of us both and posted the ad. He made a comment that we all had to have sex first since my first threesome had to be with him. I was heavily under the influence and liked to push his buttons and I jokingly said no. What happened next shook me. I was laying on the bed and he came and put his hands over my throat and started choking me. At this point I could no longer hear what he was saying. Time stood still and sped up at the same time. I froze.

When he let go, I ran into the bathroom and locked the door. I was heading into panic attack mode. I started smoking a joint right in the hotel room bathroom to calm down.

He came lightly tapping on the door, apologizing profusely. Saying he didn't mean to scare me, that I just got him so furious, and that I shouldn't push his buttons like that. The fight was terrifying when it happened, but it did save me from taking any "clients" from Billy's ad. Then we made up.

Growing up I was taught that if a man ever lays his hands on you, you leave. Get out immediately. And I honestly thought it would be that easy. I could see the potential in Billy though. His desire to make the world a better place. His dreams and aspirations. I foolishly felt I could help him.

One night he and I were at his place, a basement apartment. I don't remember the conversation we were having but I seemed to have pushed those buttons again. This time he grabbed me by my shirt and shoved me against the wall, his hands against my throat. Instead of freezing this time my body went into fight or flight mode. I scrambled and kicked until I could get away and ran to the stairs. He grabbed my leg and pulled me back down. Sheer panic spread across my body and complete terror took over.

He noticed and said he just didn't want me to leave and that he was sorry. It was too late. I went into the darkest place I had ever been. I remember curling up on the kitchen floor screaming, rocking myself back and forth as I pulled my hair out. I don't know how long I was there for. When I started to calm down I knew I had to leave but I was too high to drive. I stayed awake that whole night and left in the morning.

I tried to avoid Billy after that. He would call and send messages. He would even pretend to be someone else to call me. He would put my number on the backpage ads so I would get calls from random guys. I still felt he could change though, and that I was the one to help him. One day I was walking to work and got a call from Roxy. Billy was in jail. One of his new girls stood him up and the cops were there waiting for him at the hotel.

I visited him a few times in jail and we would write letters back and forth. Some of those letters were kind and sweet, talking about his aspirations and plans when he got out. Some of those were hurtful and mean, talking about how I ruined his life and how he would ruin mine. It got to the point when I lost all hope for him and for myself. My life had turned dark. I was always drinking or getting high. My relationship with my family was strained, and I didn't have many friends left. I was certain Billy had taken all my light, and I was worried if I would ever come out of the darkness.

That was until the most fateful day. In school we had to take a cooking class and this is where I met the most vibrant person I had ever seen. She had colourful hair in a pixie cut, and I immediately felt drawn to her. She said she did Life Activations and I knew that's exactly what I needed. I was Life Activated in May of 2016, and two months later I took the Empower Thyself Initiation.

I felt hopeful again! My light had returned stronger than ever. I met a whole new group of friends randomly one night and they quickly became my soul family. My life did a 180-degree flip. I was happy again. I started seeing the good and beauty in life. I finished school! I moved back to my hometown and got a place with my best friend!

I had no idea what this Path of Progression and The Modern Mystery School was. I just knew it was where I needed to be. I went to Healer's Academy so that I could learn how to give the Life Activation to others. Up until that point, I was in communication with Billy off and on. But after Healer's Academy, I had healed myself so much that I finally put my foot down and told him I was done. We haven't spoken since.

I continued to walk the path and more things opened up to me. I was able to heal even more. The Universal Hermetic Kabbalah program is where I discovered my purpose and finally felt I had a sense of direction. I continued walking The Path and became a Ritual Master and Guide.

My life has completely changed. I am sober and no longer use substances to hide the pain. I no longer suffer from anxiety or depression. I am filled with joy! I have been in a healthy relationship for the past 3 years with a man who treats me like a Queen. He moved in at the beginning of Covid and we spent lockdown together. He has never yelled at me, never disrespected me, never abused me in any way, even when I would try to push his buttons, (which I tried to do a lot when we first started dating). A lot of my old wounds came up (and sometimes still do), and he holds space which allows me to heal. I feel safe to communicate my insecurities, and together we are growing as individuals and as a couple. He randomly buys me flowers and kisses my forehead. We dance in the kitchen and have conversations that last hours. He is cool, calm, and collected while I am hyper and wild. He is the yin to my yang.

I have learned that relationships are our biggest mirror and where we have the greatest potential for growth. The more I healed and started to love myself, the more I was able to receive love from another. It is possible to be with someone who is the perfect fit for you. Someone who is your best friend. Someone who loves and accepts you for you, with all your quirks and insecurities. I am forever grateful for this path because it allowed me to heal and to finally realize that I am worthy of such a relationship.

And here's a little secret: so are YOU!

John's Story: Finding Love
By Jeannie Vassos

I met John when he came to one of my group Ensofic Ray Group Healing nights. He had experienced Reiki and thought he'd "check this out." He came back a few times, and then for meditation nights.

From what I could tell, he was doing well in life. He had a good, stable job as a technician for medical equipment, a nice car, friends, and was open to going to different places and experiencing new things. He was in his early thirties, handsome, intelligent, had good interpersonal/social skills and is genuinely a nice person. From an outsider's point of view, he was a "catch." He was humble and modest enough to know he had good qualities, but couldn't figure out what the missing link was. Why hadn't he found someone to share his life with?

He loved crystals and felt comfortable enough to bring some with him when he came for an event, class or healing. He said he felt they were the best choice for decorating his apartment. He even brought a few when he came to the Empower Thyself Initiation (2018). He asked such good and advanced questions during the class for some interesting discussion.

Shortly after being initiated, John went to a trade show that featured gem and crystals, and met a woman there. I remember him telling me about their meeting. How they met a one of the booths, began polite chit-chat and discovered they were both interested in spirituality, metaphysics, and energy healing, and didn't want the conversation to end. She originally comes from South America but was in Canada on a work permit. She had committed long-term employment, but as the relationship became serious very quickly seriously, they began the process of permanent residency and got married.

They now have a beautiful child and are currently living in South America. John worked for a company that manufactured specialized medical equipment, but also began to delve into something more soul-supporting: beekeeping. Just like when he talked about crystals, his face, voice and demeanor changed when he spoke about his bees and hives.

John had received the Life Activation, Full Spirit Activation, and had also attended many other classes such as Astral Travel, and the Sacred Geometry series. But he knew without a doubt that it was the Initiation that was responsible for the changes within him. He was able to release whatever was blocking him from meeting the love of his life and living a life of purpose.

Linh's Story: Breaking the Cycle of Abusive & Manipulative Relationships
By Linh Le

I was born and raised in Vietnam in a typical family with my mom, my dad, and my older brother. Well - typical from the outside. I had never had a role model for good relationships of any kind, especially romantic ones.

Ever since I was little, I could tell my parents were miserable on their own, and with each other. At some point, they could no longer hide it, and their conflicts became obvious. My brother and I quickly learned to watch out for noises of heavy steps or slammed doors, holding our breath to prepare for what was to come. As a young kid, I learned to watch out for my parents' moods so as not to receive any misdirected anger and frustration. No, my brother and I were never really abused (save for the traditional Vietnamese spanking), but we were witnesses of domestic violence. For a period of time, I lived in constant fear for mine and my mother's safety.

I grew up believing that my mom was a victim in the relationship. That led me to think that, as a woman, I had to worry for my safety, watch over my shoulder, as well as be calculated in my moves to make sure I wasn't taken advantage of. She started warning us to behave well unless we wanted to set dad off. Either that, or she would cry in front of me, comparing me to other kids, wanting me to be the bridge that harmonized my parents. Guilt and anxiety started building up within me. I felt responsible for the pain between my mom and my dad, and yet I didn't know how I could help.

It was not a surprise then, when I grew up fearing men, and at the same time, desperate for their approval. And I brought all that anxiety and fears into any relationship or even just interactions I had with any man. Obsessing over someone while pushing them away, using my body to get love, extreme jealousy, tremendous fear of being left alone, etc. - those were typical in my interactions with men.

Despite what I was taught about romantic relationships and marriage, I was always a rebel - an intuitive one at that. There was this voice in my head that constantly reminded me that THIS - everything that I was witnessing - wasn't the only way relationships were, and that whatever relationship I would be in did not have to follow that same pattern.

In 2018, I had a big spiritual awakening moment, interestingly after a breakup. Within two months afterwards, I got a Life Activation, Full Spirit Activation, and took the Empower Thyself Initiation. Even after Empower Thyself, I continued the old destructive patterns while dating men. My fears of abandonment manifested so strongly that one time, I was seeing a man living in the same building complex as me AND HE WAS STILL TOO BUSY TO SEE ME, except at 10PM. How funny it is to see the way your mind creates your reality!

As this was going on, I still believed that there is someone out there who was the right fit for me. Someone with whom I would have a beautiful relationship, beyond what I could imagine. And so for a few months, I would do a prayer every day named the "Calling Upon", listing out the qualities I was seeking in my ideal mate, and praying for my divine union partner to come sweep me off my feet.

Not seeing results after a few months, at some point I felt defeated, thinking I would have to become a perfect being to be able to meet him. And I definitely felt nowhere near perfect!

Fast forward to a few months after coming back from Healer's Academy, I started my healing practice and was doing sessions and classes, being busy with fulfilling my true purpose! For the first time (and the only time up until that point) in my life, I completely forgot about needing someone by my side. I felt joyful and fulfilled just being able to do Life Activations, and to serve, and my mind stopped even thinking about finding a mate. Lo and behold, in that exact moment, my current boyfriend appeared out of the blue! We were matchmade by our area leader - a Modern Mystery School Guide who has worked with us for years and knows us well.

Everything went so smoothly - from the first time we met, to our first date. It couldn't be more perfect than if someone wrote it in a romantic fan fiction! We were seated next to each other at the Full Moon event where we first met *by chance*. On our first date, he took me to the cat cafe I had always wanted to go (and hadn't told him), and I put my hair in a French braid which was his favorite hairstyle (which he never mentioned). In the weeks that followed, I started getting messages in my meditations and astrology reading about my husband - which has never come up before that. And he'd had dreams of me (or at least features of me) since he was in high school!

My man definitely swept me off my feet - and continues to do so. One of the things I admire the most about him is his ability to recognize and nurture the goodness in me! In the beginning of our relationship, I still held a lot of wounded feminine energies, and certain behavioral patterns still showed, such as crying hysterically, threatening to break up, or demanding him to meet certain criteria. But at that point, I finally was ready and willing to change, and he was able to meet me where I was at - holding strong boundaries that those behaviors weren't acceptable while showering me with love and compassion.

Again and again, he reminded me of my good heart and showed up for me when I needed him to, showing me what divine masculinity is supposed to be, and helping me heal that dysfunctional relationship with men. I can tell him about my darkest deepest secrets ever, and would still feel completely accepted and safe. He is one of the people in my life, along with many teachers and initiates in the Modern Mystery School, that show me how much a person (me, in this case) can change when they are totally loved and cared for. Not having their shortcomings and weaknesses criticized as a misguided expression of love, but being completely loved and accepted for who they are.

Of course, we are not without our imperfections, but I have learned what I call the formula to solving relationship issues, which has helped me well and hopefully will help you too. Out of 100% of the problems that arise in your relationships (with anyone, not just with your significant other), I think 98% are YOUR problem. They are yours in the sense that they are your own triggers and you are responsible for healing them and cleaning up your perceptions, and once you do, the problem won't be there anymore, and you do not necessarily need to talk to your partner about it.

Out of the 2% left, 1.5% are the problems you need to discuss with your partner, and together find a win-win solution. Notice I said win-win, not a compromise, which is usually a win-lose or lose-lose. This requires communication as well as commitment to making the relationship work. The last 0.5% are the problems that even after talking, you can't find solutions for. So what do you do? If you choose to be with this person, you learn to ACCEPT them where they are, UNDERSTANDING THAT THEY ARE AN EXACT REFLECTION OF YOU, whether or not you like it. And if you choose to do so, this 0.5% becomes like the 98% - they become something that YOU are responsible for healing - not healing and changing your partner, but healing yourself so you're able to accept yourself and your partner exactly where you are at - both your strengths and your weaknesses.

I am grateful that we both are initiates in The Modern Mystery School, and are dedicated to the betterment of ourselves and of the world. I feel that being on the path makes our relationship much better, as we are not easily bogged down by the common petty relationship issues. Instead, we are able to work on much deeper problems AND move through them quickly. As we also share the same mission of building world peace, we get to encourage each other and move forward together in our personal and professional lives. He is indeed my partner in service!

And of course, not only did I break the cycle of abuse and manipulations in my relationships with others (in the sense that I know I would never repeat the extremity like my parents did, nor get stuck in the behaviors), I have and continue learning to create higher human relationships - those that are based in soul and spirit connection, in harmony, love, and peace. It may be hard to imagine what that's like right now, but as you choose to walk The Mystery School path, I am confident you'll start seeing that for yourself. There aren't any words that can describe these kinds of relationships - but I, as well as many Modern Mystery School practitioners, are here to embody and show you what is possible in this physical realm!

Trevor and Jane's Story: Inner Couple's Retreat
By Brandee Downs

Trevor and Jane are a married couple from Minnesota. They are in their mid-30's and came to me for a Life Activation because they felt stuck on multiple levels. They felt stuck as a couple, as parents, and in their careers. They have been married for five years, they have three children, all girls ages ten, nine, and three. They are a blended family with Trent having the two older children from a previous marriage. Before the Life Activation, Trent was working as an electrician in the construction field and Jane was working at her daughter's day care to save money, while spending time with her.

I want to share their story as a couple because they decided to do the Life Activation as a couple. Of course, their sessions were stand-alone, but they had them done one day apart.

Before the first session with Trevor, he stated that he had struggled with feelings of depression and anxiety, which led to not feeling worthy as a husband, father, or employee. He said he wanted to progress in life. He was about to turn 38 years old, was on his second marriage, and wanted to strengthen his current marriage and make it a place of joy. He was tired of allowing his anger to take over and tired of feeling stuck.

After the session, Trevor stated he felt a weight had been lifted, and his life changed over the next 15 months. He started to observe himself in a different light and when he got upset, he could stop, observe, and ask himself why. It was like the Life Activation created space to see things from a different perspective. About a year after his Life Activation, he said, "Now, when I get upset, I can stop, look at my wife, and tell her I am sorry. Whereas before, I fed myself the excuse that I did not need to be sorry and that it was her problem. It has changed our relationship dramatically, and we communicate better."

Before Jane's session she stated she struggled with self-love and constantly compared herself to her husband's ex-wife. She struggled with knowing if she was a good step-mom and mother to her children and whether she was ready to have another baby. Her emotions were mixed, and she felt conflicted on her life journey. She had a miscarriage several months prior to her session. During our session, she felt a lot of releases, as if the stress was being lifted. Immediately after the session Jane did not have much to report but felt more at peace.

Over the next nine months, Trevor and Jane had many life changes. As a couple they started to listen to each other and communicate more openly. Jane stopped comparing herself to Trevor's ex-wife, and they started to build their relationship again. Jane was able to get pregnant and they both left their jobs and received new ones. Trevor's new job was as a sales rep for an electrician company, a job he had wanted for a long time, and it provided more financial stability for his family. With the new baby coming, and new job for rent, they sold their home and moved to a new location. Since the Life Activation they both feel like their relationship, spirituality, and parenting has strengthened.

Trevor and Jane are thankful for the shift they felt during and after the Life Activation. When I ask if they would do it again, the answer is "yes."

Five: Career and Finding Purpose

To truly know the world, look deeply within your own being; to truly know yourself, take real interest in the world.

— Rudolf Steiner

Julia's Story: Finding Her Purpose as the Matriarch of the Family
By Dawn Ressel

Julia was in her early 60s and had just moved to Florida to be closer to her family. She had been living in Ohio for a couple decades, a thousand miles apart from most of her family. She missed them so much. She had been trying for many years to move closer to them, and finally she and her husband had made it happen. They bought a home very close to her two daughters and five grandchildren.

Julia had been working for over forty years, so she naturally figured she would find a job shortly after the move. However, she wasn't really sure if she wanted to go back to the kind of work she was doing before in the food industry. It was tough on her body – long hours and standing on her feet all the time. But she thought if she took a part-time job maybe she could do it. She applied for several jobs, but nothing panned out.

Julia also considered starting her own catering company. She started getting the word out through family and friends and ended up getting a few small jobs. But it wasn't really taking off the way she wanted. She was looking for direction about what to do next and feeling unsettled about not being what she thought of as productive.

Julia heard about the Life Activation and decided to give it a try. She was open-minded about what might happen and thought it could help her navigate this crossroads in her life.

Almost immediately after the Life Activation, Julia stopped having interest in getting a part-time job or starting her own business. She started to realize that her drive to do these things was coming more from a place of habit or what she thought she had to do rather than what she really wanted at this stage of her life. She gave herself permission to not work for at least a while to see what happened. After all, she had a new house, a garden, and lots of family to spend time with.

Once Julia stopped focusing on what she needed to do for work, she started putting her energy into her family. She started spending much more time with her daughters and grandchildren. She started rebuilding the relationships that had become somewhat distant because they lived so far apart. She started seeing places where her family really needed her!

She offered to pitch in to ease some of the burden off of her daughters. She would take the kids to and from school occasionally. She would watch her grandchildren in the evenings or weekends when her daughters needed to stay at work late or wanted to have some time to themselves. She started feeling joy in seeing where she could help out and being available to do it.

One of Julia's grandsons was in middle school at the time. He was withdrawn and rarely opened up to anyone, even his parents. He was shy and reserved at school and didn't have many friends. Before Julia's Life Activation she had a really difficult time connecting with this grandson and felt unable to help him, even though she saw he was struggling.

Then after the Life Activation, Julia noticed a big shift in her relationship with this grandson. Suddenly, he started opening up to her. He would confide in her the things he was struggling with at school, with his peers, or the emotional turmoil he felt inside about his parents. His mother was divorced and remarried, and he had a distant relationship with his biological father. He started confiding in his grandmother Julia about what he was going through. He started asking for her advice. He even started taking her advice. He trusted her in a way that he had never trusted anyone before. Julia was starting to see her purpose.

Julia realized that she was in the phase of her life where it was time to claim her role as the matriarch of the family. Before the Life Activation, this was not clear to her. She didn't see that her family really needed this. And furthermore, she didn't feel called to do this. But after the Life Activation, her relationships with her family all shifted for the better. Her grandson was one example, but suddenly her daughters and her other grandchildren also drew closer to her. They started opening up to her. They started expressing the areas where they could really use more support. And it gave Julia meaning and purpose that she had been missing but didn't even realize all those years living a thousand miles apart.

It's been about four years since Julia received her Life Activation. She has settled very comfortably into her role as the family's matriarch. She does so much for her family to support them, from the day to day helping out with errands and babysitting, to being a rock of emotional support they can rely on. She organizes family get-togethers at her house regularly. She's an excellent cook, and it brings her great joy to be able to share that gift with her family. It is one of the many ways she shows her love for her family. The family is much closer than ever, and it has so much to do with Julia's presence. The Life Activation changed not only her life, but her entire family's life as a result!

Sharon's Story: From Depressed and Bed-Ridden to Living Her Mission
By Dawn Ressel

Sharon was lying in bed, pregnant, on doctor-ordered bed rest. She had been on bed rest for many months, since she first found out she was pregnant. It gave her a lot of time to think. She didn't like most of her own thoughts.

Although Sharon was grateful to be pregnant again, she was also grieving some big losses. She was in her early 40s. Her last pregnancy was stillborn. She got pregnant again soon after, but since she was high risk, it caused her to be put on bed rest. Her father recently died, which was a huge loss to her. Because she had to stay in bed, she couldn't work. She lost the job that she thought was her life purpose. She was upset about the way it ended. She felt that she had wasted years of her life, putting in so much time and effort for that job and that company, and now it appeared that it meant nothing.

Sharon's time alone to think was a blessing and a curse. She spent a lot of time in sadness and grief, depressed, even having suicidal thoughts at times. The only thing that kept her wanting to stay alive was her children. She had a son and now another one on the way. That was her main motivation to keep going. The time alone also gave her time to think about the meaning of life and her purpose.

As Sharon thought about her past and her potential future, she kept feeling there must be more to life. There must be a bigger purpose. She felt a calling to become a healer. But she had no idea how to get from her past career working for a technology company to becoming a healer. But somehow that feeling that she is meant to become a healer stayed with her. However, overall, she felt like a boat that was lost at sea. She was overtaken by the currents and didn't know how to get where she needed to go.

Sharon's son was born healthy. She was able to recover and get back to normal activities that a mother of a newborn would do, mainly caring for her child. However, during this time when her son was young she reconnected with me (a friend), and I was now a spiritual healer. She saw a post on my social media that I was going to training with The Modern Mystery School in London. Suddenly something clicked in Sharon's head. She immediately knew, this is it! This is what I've been waiting for.

Sharon reconnected with me in person and we spoke about my spiritual journey. Sharon was intrigued by my seemingly dramatic change for the better since we'd last seen each other a couple years ago. So Sharon booked her Life Activation. At this point, she felt like she didn't have anything to lose. She had tried so many other things that never worked.

During Sharon's Life Activation she felt and saw and experienced many things that were new to her and she didn't have the vocabulary to explain. She never thought of herself as psychic. But during this session she felt herself as if she was a lotus flower opening up. She'd never thought of herself like this before! She thought of herself as a practical, logical person who wants rational answers for everything. But she couldn't explain away what she was experiencing and sensing, things that were all new to her but also felt right.

After the Life Activation, Sharon's life started to gradually change for the better. The session intrigued her so much that she wanted to know more. But again, she thought of herself as a rational person. She wanted explanations for why she experienced these new things.

Luckily, the classes she took like Sacred Geometry and Astral Travel started to give her some explanations, in addition to opening her up to new experiences. She liked that the classes offered history behind them and the methods went back to King Salomon thousands of years ago. This made her feel it was grounded and proven.

After taking several classes, Sharon could see the classes were organized and based on a comprehensive system, and that it was ordered. In a way it satisfied her rational, scientific mind, but she also felt a pull that was beyond reason to keep going. It was a spiritual pull. She was tapping into her psychic gifts and intuition in a way she never had before. The tools she received in the classes were allowing her to open up to these possibilities.

Then Sharon did the Empower Thyself Initiation. It was a profoundly healing experience for her. She started to be able to see meaning in her past experiences, even the great losses she experienced with her father and stillborn child. She started to understand more of the meaning of life, and why we are here. The experiences she had up until then started to fit into a larger picture. And she learned about the path forward to fulfilling her purpose as a healer. She finally saw how it would be possible to fulfill her soul's calling. On the first day of Empower Thyself she declared that she was going to Healer's Academy to learn how to do the Life Activation for others. She was more certain and determined of this decision than she had been about anything in a long time. She couldn't explain it in rational terms. But she was absolutely sure it was the right thing to do.

Sharon asked, "When is the next Healer's Academy?" It was happening in just over two weeks in London. Here she was with a 6 month old newborn child. There were going to be lots of logistical hurdles to make it happen, but she was unwavering in her commitment.

Over the next couple of weeks before Healer's Academy, Sharon had to overcome many obstacles. Some were foreseen, such as getting childcare for over a week while she was traveling overseas. Her husband somewhat reluctantly agreed to support her on this journey. It was all happening very fast and he was unfamiliar with the Life Activation and Healer's Academy. All he knew was his wife wanted to leave their newborn for over a week to do a training he'd never heard of. It was a shock. However, after seeing Sharon's level of commitment, he agreed to support her even if he didn't understand.

Next, Sharon's sister-in-law became an obstacle. She objected very loudly to Sharon's wish to go to Healer's Academy. She tried to make Sharon believe she was being manipulated into going. She questioned what seemed to her like a sudden change of career choice. She hadn't noticed that over the past several months since Sharon's Life Activation and spiritual growth that she had become a new person. She was used to a version of Sharon that was passive and went along with what other people told her to do. She was used to a version of Sharon that was easily swayed by other's opinions and was very impressionable. It was out of love and concern that Sharon's sister-in-law expressed very strong doubts about this decision. However, she was wrong.

Over the past six months Sharon had come to know herself more clearly than she ever had. She had come to trust her own intuition and judgment. She had become much more solid in what she wanted over what others told her she should want. She had received teachings that the people around her hadn't received. The teachings gave her confidence in her choices and a purpose for her actions. And it was from this place that she decided to go to Healer's Academy.

Though it was hard to stand up to her sister-in-law who was an opinionated and forceful opponent, she did it. Sharon did not back down.

About a week before she was set to fly to London, Sharon's cornea got scratched. Her doctor said he didn't know if she would be able to fly in that condition. However, Sharon still did not waver in her belief. When it was time to get on the plane, she had healed well enough to fly. She overcame every obstacle and made it there. These obstacles forced her to affirm her commitment and belief in herself and her choices.

In Healer's Academy, Sharon felt so at home and at peace. She could feel so much healing happening for herself and the others in class with her. There was so much information that she had been waiting for that connected her to her purpose as a healer. She was like a sponge, soaking it all in – the new information, the energy, the healing.

In Healer's Academy they tell you that your mission as a Life Activation Practitioner is to help people and influence the collective for the better. By the end of the training, Sharon felt so empowered to help change the world.

After Healer's Academy Sharon started practicing as a healer and she started to grow in her confidence in her own abilities and that this was in fact her purpose in life. She continued to study with The Modern Mystery School. She began watching the show *"Mystery Teachings"* by Dr. Theresa Bullard on Gaia TV. The way Dr. Theresa explained the connections between spirituality and science really resonated with her. She watched every episode and still wanted more. So, when the opportunity arose to take Universal Hermetic Ray Kabbalah in person with Dr. Theresa Bullard, she jumped at the chance.

The 10-month Kabbalah program allowed Sharon to go really deep into both the study and experience of spirituality in a way she had been craving. She was looking for something to fill in the missing pieces of her understanding, and Kabbalah did that exponentially. And not only that, she learned how to live and apply this new knowledge, taking it far beyond book learning into wisdom through living it.

It's been 3 years since Sharon received her Life Activation. When she reflects back on who she was then to who she is now, she is a totally different person. Three years ago she was lost. She didn't understand her place in the world. She was suffering deeply and could find no meaning in any of it. She felt like a victim. She got offended and triggered very easily. She didn't believe in herself or have confidence in her own decisions. She didn't have any motivation to live the second half of her life other than to take care of her children. She knew she had a bigger purpose, but she had no idea how she could ever get there.

Today Sharon is living congruent with her purpose. She knows who she is and she is excited about who she is becoming – more and more of her true divine self. She gets triggered much less often. However, now when she gets triggered, she realizes it is an opportunity to examine where she still needs some healing. She has moved from feeling like a victim to taking responsibility for her own emotions and reactions.

Sharon is excited about life. She feels privileged to have the spiritual knowledge that she has received through The Modern Mystery School. She takes that privilege and responsibility seriously and knows she is meant to use it to help people and make the world better.

Sharon went from being lost at sea to being the captain of the ship. The ship is her life and she is the driver. She knows her path and she is building the path. Not only is she steering her own ship, but she's also guiding other people as a healer.

Now when Sharon imagines herself at sea, as the captain of her ship, she is not afraid of the currents. She knows that even if she hits a rock, she will recover. She is resilient. She believes in herself and her own power to overcome obstacles. She knows she has the skill and tools to navigate any situation and reach her ultimate destination.

Dean's Story: The Win to Freedom
By Brandee Downs

Dean is a 45-year-old male who is married with eight children. They range in age from 3 to 21 years old. He is a high school football coach and loves helping coach youth to step into their power. Dean received his first Life Activation in 2017, and with this, he felt more grounded, aware, and connected to the energy around him. He started to decipher his own energy and when he was picking up on other people's energy. This enhanced gift has helped him connect on the field with his team and know what his team members needed from him. It has also helped him connect with his children.

About a year and a half ago, in 2021, Dean retired from his job in Law Enforcement and, for the first time, could not provide for his family the same way he had. Even though his wife agreed to take on the responsibility of finances to allow him to step into a new life journey as a football coach, an inner conflict started to arise. Without a definite purpose, he began to feel stuck and depressed and felt like he was not providing for his family the way he wanted. He continued to push and worked extremely hard for a company as a head coach, dedicating hours of his time coaching, but he was getting paid minimally for his efforts. In 2022 he decided to get another Life Activation and the Full Spirit Activation.

Dean said after the Life Activation, his perspective of things started to change, how he reacted to other people's 3D responses began to shift, and he was more aware of what others wanted and what he needed. Within a few weeks, he left the job as a head coach that was paying a minimal wage; he received a new job offer to work in the school he now coaches at; he received a business opportunity, and he started to develop his business plan. It was like his whole life shifted to match his dreams. He began to remember his worth and what he provides for his family. He stepped into a new lifestyle, envisioning how he will start to be able to provide more for his family.

His wife reports, "after the Life Activation, my husband's joy came back, I can see his smile again, and that brings me joy. Not only is his smile back, but he has gained clarity and seems to have a solid direction in life again." His Life Activation is still in the works as it occurred just over six weeks ago as of the time of this writing.

Six: Overcoming Addiction

"Although the world is full of suffering, it is also full of the overcoming of it."

- Helen Keller

Tanya's Story: Life-Long Effects of Addiction Deeply Shifted
By Casey O'Connell

Tanya is one of those people that I met and felt an immediate kindredness. She was always deeply thoughtful and kind, and clearly incredibly sensitive to those around her. It was therefore, no surprise, when I found out that she had struggled with marijuana addiction for a huge portion of her life. Having a young son, and a blossoming life at the age of 40, it was only fitting that she wanted to move through what continued to hold her back.

I say that it was no surprise to me because I am also someone who has struggled with addiction for many years, so the assistance through the kind of trauma which causes addiction as well as the trauma done by addiction itself is near and dear to me. And I can truthfully spot it a mile away. Many people utilize substance addiction as a way to escape being as sensitive as Tanya was, seemingly for her entire life.

When she finally agreed to the Spiritual Drug Detox Series with me, I was overwhelmed with excitement for her because I knew that it would be a complete game changer. The thing about the Drug Detox series is that it doesn't just address the addiction itself, but the spiritual cause of addiction at its deepest levels.

To say that this 10-session series was a fight, is an absolute understatement. The amount of resistance that Tanya needed to work through within herself to keep meeting me halfway in the process of her healing was incredible - and she persisted! She persisted because week after week, every time we'd meet, she would share with me just how profoundly different she felt in her soul - as though mountains were moving within her. Each week, I could see the change in her eyes. The meekness with which she had previously approached the world was dissipating. The power which she had long withheld was starting to break out without apology. She was beginning to choose herself first and was learning how to say no and to set boundaries with people in her life. A tremendous step.

Each week, we would peel back the layers of what had caused her to fall into addiction and heal the core - reminding Tanya of who she truly is as a god being. Each week, she would open her eyes at the end of the session and hold my hands with tears in her eyes, thanking me for holding her in her vulnerability and shadows.

When we finally completed the 10th session, and closed up and sealed off the energies that were fueling her addictive behavior and thoughts, she noted how quiet it was in her mind. With a deep breath, she acknowledged that life would never be the same. She even noted, "this (the series) is so much more powerful than addiction."

Now, Tanya is not someone who was in active substance abuse when I met her, but this doesn't mean that the addictive thoughts and tendencies weren't still there. This series has clearly made huge impact on how her mind operates, how she views herself within the world as well as her ability to create new things and make different choices.

Where I saw an immensely powerful yet fearful woman, I now see an unstoppable force of light embodied in a Goddess, ready to take on anything in her path. Where I saw someone constantly seeking permission, I now see someone willing to make her own choices and draw her own boundaries in order to create a better life for her and her son.

I am eternally grateful to have had the opportunity to work with Tanya and to witness her transformation through the Spiritual Drug Detox Series. She truly showed up for herself, and allowed the energies and thoughts that hooked her addictively to be healed. And in doing so created the space within herself to show up and serve as who she really is.

Experiences like this is why I do what I do and they are what keeps me going even when things get tough. Deeply sensitive people are often the most prone to addictive tendencies and also the most prone to avoid putting their own healing first, which puts them in a tough spot. Yet, with modalities such as the Spiritual Drug Detox within the Lineage of King Salomon, this healing and progression is possible!

Davis' Story: Remarkable Recovery from Meth and Heroin Addiction

My story is not so different from many American families today. My younger brother, Davis, is a sensitive soul. When we were growing up, he was sweet, caring, empathetic, and fiercely loyal to his friends. He saw it as his duty to soothe the pain of people around him, even when it wasn't his responsibility, and he wanted to make the world a more comfortable place to live in. My brother was loving and wanted to be loved in return. As a child, he had good friends around him – all very clean cut, wholesome and interested in skateboarding and the outdoors.

When Davis was a teenager, he fell away from his old friends and made new ones who were more exciting to him; they were interested in smoking weed and partying. At this time, the opioid epidemic was sweeping across the country and was affecting many American families with no experience dealing with heroin and methamphetamine.

Davis wanted to be good at something. In the years that he gave his love to others, he lacked in giving it to himself. He had surrounded himself with people who did not have his best interest at heart and who used drugs to feel more excitement or to escape. Davis once said to me that he was good at smoking weed. He was the last one standing at parties and could always function to a certain degree and stay at a paid part-time job no matter how hard he partied the night before.

When all of his friends began to experiment with heavier stuff like heroin and meth, this was the next step for Davis. He never meant to get addicted, but he did. I knew something was off with my brother whenever I spoke to him on the phone. He could not hold a conversation with me whenever I called and when I saw him in person, he would hardly make eye contact.

I missed the closeness I had with my brother when we were children, but addiction made him a shell of the kind-hearted man I knew he was.

At the time, I had been studying with the Modern Mystery School for several years and had attended Healer's Academy to learn how to do the Life Activation for others. I remembered how much the Life Activation had helped me when I was battling severe anxiety and depression. I made a promise that I would give a Life Activation to Davis the next time I saw him. When I visited home, Davis consented to have the Life Activation. When he was sitting in the chair receiving the activation, I remember he hardly moved. I had no idea if he had felt anything, but I was hopeful that some light went in. I felt heartbroken about the state that my brother was in, and I was very afraid of losing him.

A few months went by, and I went home to visit once again. I was so happy to see that Davis was brighter. He and I were able to have longer conversations than we had had over the last few years. Davis had become much more interested in spirituality and was quietly still using. My whole family had found out that he had become an addict over the years, so this was no longer a secret. He knew at this point, that everyone was on to him.

Even though you only need the Life Activation once, I asked him if he wanted to try it again and he agreed. This time, the Life Activation was very different. Davis felt everything! I needed to work very slowly with most of the energy balancing as his energetic body responded to every touch and every movement. During the balancing of his energetic structure, I was surprised to see that Davis physically moved with the flow of my hands. At the end of the second Life Activation, I was overjoyed to see how much he felt it! It was surprising for me to see how sensitive my brother really was to the subtle energies. I was so excited to see what was to come.

Shortly thereafter, Davis decided to get sober. He went to detox and an inpatient rehab center. He was prescribed dopamine blockers that prevented him from getting high again. He went through physical, emotional, and mental withdrawals. Sobriety for the addict is not an easy feat. Davis pulled away from all his acquaintances, dealers, and the people he surrounded himself with and was incredibly lonely. All of the suppressed emotions, bad thoughts, and feelings that Davis had never dealt with had begun to emerge. The drugs had suppressed everything. Davis told me that to the addict, the only thing that matters is the next high. He didn't have to deal with, confront, or work through anything when he was using.

Davis worked hard and was committed to his sobriety. He stayed strong when all of the sadness and feelings of loss and remorse came to the surface. Every time I spoke to Davis, he told me how his body hurt physically and how difficult it was to deal with all of the unhappiness that he had suppressed for years. Sure enough, as time passed, things got easier for Davis. He had committed to making his life better and he took steps every day to do so.

I gave my brother the Life Activation six years ago; everything has changed since then. Davis has been sober from meth and heroin since shortly after receiving the Life Activation, and his life has completely changed. I have my brother back! My brother has returned to being the gentle, kind-hearted man he always was. Now in his early thirties, Davis committed himself to jiu-jitsu and has his purple belt with three stripes. He has a steady job working for the county Parks Department. After many years of feeling very alone, Davis told me recently that he now had so many friends he could hardly keep track of everyone. He re-built the trust with his friends, family, coworkers and most importantly, himself.

Seven: Spiritual Growth

"Humanity looked in awe upon the beauty and the everlasting duration of creation. The exquisite sky flooded with sunlight. The majesty of the dark night lit by celestial torches as the holy planetary powers trace their paths in the heavens in fixed and steady metre – ordering the growth of things with their secret infusions."

— Hermes Trismegistus

Linh's Story: From Atheist to Spiritual Guide
By Linh Le

Even though I accepted my intuitive abilities at a young age, I had always been a staunch atheist. It was partly because I was very sensitive as a child, and I could feel the energies of the people around me. I could sense their suffering and their pain. Even though they may not have said anything, I could hear their screams and cries within. It was very hard as I didn't know how to separate myself from their energies; and internalizing everything was the only thing I could do. Seeing the world through the lenses of suffering plus all the news about wars and pain everywhere, it was hard to accept that there was such a thing as God. If God does exist, why would bad things happen to good people?

I think the main reason I was an atheist though, was because of an experience I went through as a 5 year old.

These memories had always been suppressed so deep they used to only come back as flashes - like dreams or fears - but I knew that they were true. When I was 5, I was repeatedly touched by some boys in my kindergarten class. I remember being forced to kiss them. I remember the wetness and the sloppiness. I remember not knowing what to do, and as it happened during our nap times, the only thing I could do was to pretend that I was sleeping, and try to turn the other way. I remember one time overhearing the three of them deciding on whose turn it is to have fun with me that day. I remember hearing their laughter and the voices of my teachers who were watching us at nap time, and me desperately wanting them to do something. I remember not telling my parents, because they already seemed miserable enough on their own, and with each other. I didn't want to add to their burdens.

I remember lying down somewhere, feeling completely paralyzed, while others got to violate my body. No one came to the rescue. This was the moment I closed my heart to God, despite being deeply connected before that. My young brain couldn't understand why these horrible things were happening to me, if such a beautiful and powerful entity such as God truly existed.

Before I turned 25, I had my spiritual awakening moment. Despite not accepting God, because I was intuitive, I was able to follow my inner guidance to continue taking the steps in my progression. I received the Life Activation, and took the Empower Thyself Initiation within a month of each other, and I attempted to go to Healer's Academy just two months later. When the obstacles to get to Healer's Academy presented themselves (as you will find presented at every class and session with the MMS), I desperately tried everything I knew to make it happen. At some point, I asked for higher guidance on what I needed to do to move through, and I was told that it was time to accept my traumas. The visions and sensations that I'd passed off as only dreams were real - I knew it - and it was time I at least acknowledged that they were there. It wasn't an easy thing to do, and I didn't make it to Healer's that time. Nor another time a month later. I eventually made it to Healer's Academy after two tries. But it wasn't until the last weekend of my first Universal Hermetic Ray Kabbalah program more than a year later where I finally admitted and faced my anger and resentment towards God.

I cried, and cried, and was humbled. I told my class of 30+ people of my pain. And it was at that moment I finally felt I was consciously healing my relationship with God. Of course, I had been doing that the previous 2 years on The Mystery School path, but I didn't want to accept it. And I didn't have to – because God and Hierarchy of Light will meet you where you are at, not where they want you to be. I only started healing my relationship with God when I myself was ready.

3.5 years, 3 Universal Kabbalah programs, many healings and initiations later, I am now a Third Step Ritual Master and a Guide in the lineage. I have made my commitments to God - to represent God in the physical and to plant and nurture the seeds of divinity in others. I talk to God every day. My deepest desire is to stay connected and to be in alignment with this beautiful being that represents the highest and best aspects of ME. While I am sure there are still aspects of my relationship with God that need healing, I can proudly "get out of the closet" and say "I work for God!" Because of my own experience, I have come to view atheists not as those who reject God, but those who are just seeking authentic divinity.

To end this story, I want to leave you with a quick story that was a profound lesson. I was at an airport one time, trying to check in but the line was so long. When it was my turn, the airport attendant had trouble figuring out something in the system. I thought to myself, "Dear God, please help me get through this so I can get on that plane." Two seconds later, an attendant at the booth next door turned to her and asked how he could help. And he was able to help so quickly I got all my paperwork straightened out right away and rushed to the security gate! I kept laughing inside my head because that was such a powerful reminder that God is all of us and is in all of us! We are all gods and goddesses in training - we each embody different aspects of the divine. Because of that, when God acts, it is through OUR actions and thoughts.

Yes, what happened to me was terrible - I knew God wanted to show up, but unfortunately as a human being, I wouldn't. Yes, we live in a harsh world with some things happening that maybe shouldn't happen. That makes it even more important for those of us who are ready to wake up and to persistently follow our higher purpose. When we do so, we bring more of God and divinity down to the physical, and hopefully one day, no one will have to go through some of the heartbreaking traumas that we've gone through. Hopefully, one day, true peace will be anchored here on Earth. I know it can happen because it's happened to me!

Annemarie's Story: From Hating Life to Loving Life
By Dawn Ressel

Annemarie felt stuck. She was going through an existential crisis. She wondered regularly, "Why am I here? Why was I even born?" Her mind was filled with cynicism. She had so many negative thoughts and she spent a lot of time ruminating about the past, which led to a downward spiral of depression. Her mind was focused on the minor irritants of life. When she spoke to her friends they all felt the same way. She didn't see any way out. She wondered, "Is this all there is to life?"

Then in 2020 when Covid hit, it got worse. In the forced isolation she had nowhere else to go but to face her own reality. She wished she were dead. She thought about death a lot. She would drive to work and think, "I wish a truck would hit me." She hated her life.

In 2021 she started seeking a way out of the darkness. She starting exploring spiritual practices like numerology, astrology, and Kabbalah. She started working with crystals and felt a huge pull towards them. She finally started to see some relief from her negative thoughts and was able to feel more grounded by working with crystals. It started to give her hope and pushed her forward in seeking.

She found the show *"Mystery Teachings"* by Dr. Theresa Bullard of The Modern Mystery School. In one of the episodes she learned about the Life Activation modality and it piqued her interest. She found my website as a local Life Activation practitioner. She told me that once she saw my picture on the website, she felt so comfortable with me. She couldn't shake the feeling this was something she was supposed to do. So she booked the appointment.

Immediately after the Life Activation on the drive home, she felt so excited, so full of energy and childish joy. These were feelings she hadn't felt in a very long time. The next day she woke up and felt like she was seeing everything new for the first time. The colors were more vibrant. The details of the trees and flowers were so vivid. She was much more present than ever before.

Beyond the revitalized feelings and renewed sense of awe in life, she started to take stock of the habits that were holding her back. She had much more awareness of what was in alignment with who she wanted to be and what wasn't. This awareness drove her to seek the next step on the path, which was the Empower Thyself Initiation.

The Empower Thyself Initiation exposed her to concepts that were foreign to her, and at first her mind had trouble accepting it. But her heart felt open and it felt right. There was an immediate acceptance and peace within her heart that she'd never felt with other teachings. The energy and meditations in the class were very powerful. Even though her mind could not quite catch up at first, she had a feeling at her core about the truth of these teachings and the power of the methods.

It's been about one year since Annemarie completed the Empower Thyself Initiation. She feels like a totally different person. When she reads journal entries from 1-2 years ago they seem like they were written by a different person. She doesn't remember now what it's like to feel that bad. She doesn't remember what it's like to be that anxious or depressed. She has the memories of those times, but the emotional charge is gone.

Now Annemarie loves her life! She puts time and effort into her spiritual progression on a daily basis. She practices the meditations and rituals she learned in Empower Thyself daily.

She does yoga every day. Every day she reads at least one chapter of a book that will help her with her spiritual progression.

Through her work with these practices, she has developed a much greater sense of awareness of how her thoughts affect her physical and mental state. She can just be. She has an understanding of the "I AM." She understands that in the now there is peace. She has also given up all substances – all drugs and alcohol. She realizes that she was using those as a means to escape her life. And now she loves life so much there is no reason to escape. She is excited for the next steps in her spiritual journey and where they will take her.

Epilogue

I sat in meditation, tears streaming down my face, as I contemplated what to write in this epilogue. These were tears of gratitude for the life I have. I've been able to create the life I have today because of the tools of the lineage of King Salomon, handed down through The Modern Mystery School.

During our wrap-up meeting for this book my editor said, "It says a lot about the school that you got from who you were before to who you are now. And it also says a lot about you." It's fair to say that she's correct on both counts. These tools are quite simply miraculous, as the title of the book proclaims. But it is in the seeking of and application of these tools by the individual that the miracles become manifest. We are the drivers of our own healing process.

The process of writing this book was joyful, rewarding, and illuminating. I feel incredibly honored to have been entrusted by God, the Hierarchy of Light, and the contributors of this book to steer this ship to its destination.

Only a few months ago, I did not think I had the skills or experience to write a book. That was until this book came knocking on my door, almost quite literally. I meditated upon whether I should proceed, and the answer was clear. Now is the time! We are living in an era where people desperately need hope.

The problems this book addresses are some of the biggest problems facing individuals today. So many people are seeking the answers that this book may provide. This book is a conduit and a lifeline. I quickly realized that this project is bigger than me. Though I was facilitating the process into physical reality, it was being directed within the spiritual realms.

I am moved by the support I received from our community of lightworkers to make this book happen. This is the character of our community. We support and help each other towards a common mission. I want to acknowledge the hard work of the foreword author, Carla Weis, M.D., and all of the contributors. They helped create this book because they believe what I believe: that the more people who are made aware of these stories, the more people we can help!

There is not a person on the planet who has had a problem-free life. We may look from the outside and judge and think that a person had "advantages" or "had it easy." But the truth is, we have no idea what anyone else has really gone through. It's stories like these that help remind us of our common humanity. I hope that these stories will help instill more compassion and kindness towards our fellow human beings.

The people I admire the most are people who have been through difficult times and yet do not succumb to the idea that they are victims. They do not stay stuck. They look at themselves in the mirror honestly and take responsibility for their state. They do the hard work needed in order to heal. My fellow Guides in The Modern Mystery School are, without exception, this type of person. And they have gone even further than this. They climbed the mountain, and rather than simply marching forward and fending for themselves, they reached a hand backwards to help others up that mountain.

All of that being said, I think it's important to head-on address a topic that one could easily find with a Google search. The Modern Mystery School has been (falsely) accused of being a cult. I emphatically declare that this is untrue.

There has never been a cult in history that has helped people become more empowered, helped them heal, and become stronger. Our school encourages people to seek their own answers within, and then teaches them how to do so. Students exercise free will in every decision related to their involvement with the organization. If we choose to continue, it's because the tools bear positive fruit in our lives: more joy, freedom, clarity, peace, better health, and so on.

My own direct experience was all the proof I needed to be certain that these accusations were absurd. Yet, as these accusations became public, I was so impressed with how the leaders of the school and my colleagues responded. They did not do what organizations often do when they are publicly accused of wrongdoing. They did not cower. They did not make an empty apology. (Because there's no need to apologize when you haven't done anything wrong. And a false apology lacks integrity!) They did not simply sit by and wait for it to "go away." They fought back! They fought back with one of the best weapons the light has against the dark: the truth! Because in the light, the truth will remain, and the lies will shatter.

In response to the false accusations, hundreds of students posted online about their positive experiences with The Modern Mystery School and shared heartfelt thanks for how much it has changed their life for the better. Dozens of my colleagues publicly countered accusations of events that *supposedly* took place while they were present. They said things like, "I was there! That simply did NOT happen!"

Founder Gudni Gudnason, in the midst of a battle with cancer, kept working tirelessly to pass on as much knowledge as possible while ill. Our lineage holders and leaders kept working, harder than ever, even while having their reputations attacked. The leaders of The Modern

Mystery School are the most dedicated people of the highest integrity that I have ever met. They are living proof that the tools of our lineage do indeed work!

This is why discernment is key. We live in a society where mere accusations are often accepted as fact. This is quite frankly a dangerous society to live in! Those who have an agenda to get more clicks for their tabloid are sometimes believed over those working selflessly to serve others. This should give pause to anyone with critical thinking skills and anyone who values justice and fairness.

If there is selfishness in the work we do as practitioners in The Modern Mystery School, it is this: we know that each person who heals makes the world better. And we know that we are all connected. One person at a time, starting with ourselves, we work to make this world better - because that's the world we want to live in!

"It is not the critic who counts; not the man who points out how the strong man stumbles, or where the doer of deeds could have done them better. The credit belongs to the man who is actually in the arena, whose face is marred by dust and sweat and blood; who strives valiantly; who errs, who comes short again and again, because there is no effort without error and shortcoming; but who does actually strive to do the deeds; who knows great enthusiasms, the great devotions; who spends himself in a worthy cause; who at the best knows in the end the triumph of high achievement, and who at the worst, if he fails, at least fails while daring greatly, so that his place shall never be with those cold and timid souls who neither know victory nor defeat." – Theodore Roosevelt

In the spirit of this famous quote by Theodore Roosevelt, we should put a lot more trust in those who have actually entered the arena and have dared greatly by doing so. I hope that this book inspires you to step into the arena and go further into the rewarding journey of your own healing.

Some of the contributors to this book shared their own stories, which required bravery and vulnerability. Some shared details of their lives that they had never openly shared before. As did I. We did so in hopes that we may reach someone who is dealing with something similar. That person may think they are alone or that there is no hope. But we are proof that there is hope – because we were there, and we overcame it!

One thing I've learned about suffering is that we can make meaning out of it. Overcoming suffering makes us stronger. It makes us more resilient. It makes us more grateful for what we have. Overcoming suffering puts us in a better position to help others, if we so choose.

I do not linger in regret about the decades of suffering I experienced because of anxiety disorder. Now that I'm on the other side of it, I see that it served a purpose: to get me to where I am now – living joyfully and gratefully! And it allows me to be an example to others who are struggling with this condition. It was extremely difficult, but I've found meaning in it. It drives me to do what I do.

The stories in this book help shed light on the gamut of problems we can begin to tackle by reconnecting people with their spiritual essence and their creator. This is not about the God from religion. It is free from dogma. This is about acknowledging that we all come from the same divine source, and therefore, we are also divine!

The motto of the ancient mystery schools is to "Know Thyself." This lineage is about helping people to remember more of who they truly are: the powerful creator of their own life. This is quite a feat in a world designed to make us forget. We are constantly sold the idea that in order to fill the void we feel inside, we need things outside of ourselves. But in this lineage, we help people remember that what they are seeking exists within.

Reading these stories and seeing them come together as a collection has further strengthened my commitment to this work. It was only a few short years ago that I myself was drowning in the problems of this world. It is a privilege to share these possible solutions to many of the issues people currently face. If this book helps even one person to gain healing from these methods to the degree that I have, it will have been worth it. Perhaps that person will be you!

I'm so grateful that you have chosen to read this book. I wish you the fullest life and the most joy possible, dear reader, no matter what path you choose to get there.

About The Author

Dawn Ressel is a certified Guide, Healer, Teacher, and Life Activation practitioner with The Modern Mystery School and the Owner of The Light Within. She holds a Master's Degree in Digital Media from Georgia Institute of Technology and a Bachelor's Degree in Communications from Florida State University.

Dawn teaches metaphysical classes, meditation, and offers private healing sessions in San Diego. She is also a Ritual Master, Initiated Celtic Shaman, and Kabbalist in the Universal Hermetic tradition.

Dawn began her spiritual journey in 2014 while seeking a way to overcome her lifelong struggle with generalized anxiety disorder. Now having completely healed, she assists others on their path of spiritual progression, healing, and empowerment.

Dawn's purpose and vision is to help others create a life of joy, meaning, and empowerment. She believes that each person who heals themselves creates a ripple effect on their family, community, and the collective. She believes that we are all connected, and that the best way to serve humanity is to start by healing ourselves.

Dawn lives in the city of San Diego, California with her two cats: Ivy and Sol.

Contact Information

Please contact Dawn Ressel at:

The Light Within

Address:
8885 Rio San Diego Dr., Suite 237
San Diego, CA 92108

E-mail: dawn@lightwithinheal.com

Website: www.lightwithinheal.com

Facebook: www.facebook.com/lightwithinheal

Instagram: www.instagram.com/dawnressel

Services offered

- Private energy healing sessions

- Meditation coaching

- Metaphysical classes

- Initiation into the lineage of King Salomon

Contributor Bios

Dr. Kate Bartram Brown has a PhD in Natural Medicine and is the Head of Modern Mystery School Europe UK & EU. Kate is the CEO of globally successful business Mini Me Yoga which recently received an award from HRH the Princess Royal for excellence in training. She is passionate about serving humanity and helping others create success in all areas of their lives. After healing herself from cancer in her late 20's, then creating a success global company by walking the path of the lineage of King Salomon, she is dedicated her life to sharing these hidden sciences with others.
www.modernmysteryschooluk.com
kate@modernmysteryschooluk.com

Amber Campbell is a certified Teacher, Healer and Guide within the Lineage of King Salomon. She is also a Certified Nutritional Practitioner from the Institute of Holistic Nutrition. Amber has found her passion in helping to empower others to live and create a life they love through the healings and teachings with the Modern Mystery School.
www.ambercampbell.co
info@ambercampbell.co
1-705-441-5386
Collingwood Ontario, Canada

Karla Clark of Urban Magick and SoulScience. MMS Certified Guide, Teacher, Healer, Kabbalist, Wiccan Priestess, Magus Hermeticus, Ensofic Ray Practitioner, and King Salomon Healer. Karla began as a research scientist and anthropologist; she bridges the fields of science and metaphysics. Experience true clarity, joy, and deep, lasting, transformational healing utilizing the purest metaphysical tools available. Co-create a thorough and clear plan for your progression – deep healings, deep teachings, and regular practice. Live from a place of power and choice.
www.urbanmagick.net
Karla@urbanmagick.net
206-227-3520
2801 Camino Del Rio S., San Diego, CA 92108

Brandee Downes is a Teacher and Healer with the Modern Mystery School. She has been a Life Activation Practitioner since 2017. She has a diverse background as a Marriage and Family Therapy, 20 years of military experience, and is retired with 14 years in Law Enforcement. Brandee has studied spirituality for 31 years. Through the Divine Awakening Center in Farmington, Utah, she looks forward to serving her Modern Mystery School clients each week and watching their flowers bloom. Her contact information is available at https://divineawakeningcenter.com/brandee-downes

Christine Estrema M.S. is a Healer, Teacher and Guide in the Lineage of King Salomon with the Modern Mystery School. She holds a Master's Degree in Cardiovascular Science and did Biomedical Research for 14 years at UC San Diego, UC San Francisco and in Bio-tech. Christine works with those who are looking to bridge science and spirituality within themselves to find healing and greater fulfillment in life. Her mission is to help people know themselves so that they can live with integrity of who they really are, cultivate their own direct connection to God, and create a life of inner peace, self love and JOY!
www.burnbrightlylife.com
hello@christineestrema.com
(737) 888-5563
Austin, TX

Linh Le helps motivated individuals learn to trust and love themselves by gaining a deeper understanding of their individuality, divinity, and innate goodness. We aren't always able to see ourselves in the highest light, and in this society, self-compassion and self-trust are often overlooked. That's where I come in and work with you one-on-one to create a personalized plan to help you take back your power and learn to see the best in yourself and others!
Magick of Choice
linh@magickofchoice.com
www.magickofchoice.com
347-815-3605
IG: @magickofchoice
YouTube: Magick of Choice
San Francisco, CA

Phyllis Francene Livera graduated from Felician College and holds a BSN. She re-entered nursing during COVID and works part time and per diem in a rehab center in Lebanon, New Jersey. She practices healing And Reiki at her center. She is a certified Healer, Teacher, and Guide granted by the Modern Mystery School International. Handed down in the sacred lineage of King Salomon.
Healing Power
172 Washington Valley Rd Suite #3
Warren, NJ 07059

Casey O'Connell is a Teacher, Healer and Guide in the Lineage of King Salomon with The Modern Mystery School. She helps sensitive souls to embrace their magick and find safety in their unique abilities so they can truly live here on Earth.
Her mission is to help humans remember the wonder and goodness within our direct connection to God through ancient initiation, activation, healing, and ceremony.
www.caseyoconnell.net
Caseyoco@gmail.com
512-545-7522
1010 Land Creek Cove, Suite 100, Austin, TX 78746

Lorraine Pimienta has been studying with the Modern Mystery School since 2010 and is a Guide, Teacher and Healer within the Lineage of King Salomon. She offers private 1:1 healing sessions and metaphysical classes in Orange County, California and is passionate about helping others enhance their lives with the Lineage teachings.
www.thiseuphoriclife.com
lorraine4mms@gmail.com
www.facebook.com/thiseuphoriclife
www.instagram.com/thiseuphoriclife
949-550-3228

Jeannie Vassos. I am an agent for World Peace. By continually striving to be my best self, I experience more inner peace. My mission is to share the knowledge, tools, and wisdom from the Royal Lineage of King Salomon to help you achieve your highest and best quality of life, and therefore to create a better world for everyone. Jeannie is located in Newmarket, Ontario, Canada. Contact her through her website or Facebook www.themiddlepillar.ca or www.facebook.com/themiddlepillar or by phone at 905-717-5907

Carla Weis, MD is a certified Healer, Teacher and Guide in the lineage of King Salomon and owner of Sacred Vibrations, LLC. She received her M.D. from Temple University School of Medicine in Philadelphia, PA and practiced as a board-certified neonatologist for 30 years, caring for the smallest of patients in NICU's in Pennsylvania, New Jersey, Georgia, Hawaii and California. She has received advanced spiritual training from the Modern Mystery School since 2011 and now focuses her time on assisting and guiding others in their own spiritual progression, creating a sacred and safe space for all. She believes that life is meant to be lived, and that realizing your own true potential is part of thriving as a spiritual and physical being.

www.sacred-vibrations.com

sacredvibrations33@gmail.com

Huntington Beach, CA

Charitable Donations

A portion of the sales of this book will be donated to the 501(c)(3) nonprofit The San Diego Food Bank. The Jacobs & Cushman San Diego Food Bank and our North County Food Bank chapter provide nutritious food to people in need, advocate for the hungry, and educate the public about hunger-related issues.

The Jacobs & Cushman San Diego Food Bank and our North County Food Bank chapter comprise the largest hunger-relief organization in San Diego County. In 2021, the Food Bank distributed 63 million pounds of food, and the Food Bank serves, on average, 500,000 people per month in San Diego County.

Through our North County Food Bank chapter and by partnering with nearly 500 nonprofit partners with feeding programs, the Food Bank provides nutritious food to individuals and families in need in communities throughout San Diego County.

About The Lineage Of King Salomon

Lineage is a key factor in determining the authenticity, power, and authority of a mystery school. The lineage of King Salomon is the lineage held and taught by The Modern Mystery School. The unbroken lineage can be verified and traced back to King Salomon himself, over 3,000 years ago. However, the mystery school traditions are much older than that, and some of the teachings go back at least 8,000 years to Hermes.

This lineage has persisted over several millennia through the ancient tradition of sharing knowledge from teacher to student, affirmed by the holy process of initiation. The direct transfer of knowledge in this fashion, in addition to an unbroken line of lineage holders has insured the integrity and virtue of this tradition. The mystery schools have held the secrets of God, the universe, and the keys to true spiritual power since the beginning of time.

During his time, King Salomon brought together healers, shamans, and medicine people from indigenous tribes all over the planet. They studied and practiced together in his temple, which was really a full city, for 20-40 years. And they tested the healings from all over the world. King Salomon wanted to create a universal system of healings and teachings. Meaning it worked for all people, all the time, regardless of genetics or location. From these decades of work, we have the most comprehensive system of healings and empowerment on the planet. These are the King Salomon healing modalities.

King Salomon knew there would be a time in history when everyday people would be ready for these teachings, activations, and healings. He knew there would be a time where people would awaken and they would need tools. That time is now. His purpose was to share these healings and the mystery school teachings with all.

In this current age, The Modern Mystery School is the only one of the seven ancient mystery schools that is open to the public. The integrity of our lineage is of utmost importance. We preserve this lineage through methods that include but are not limited to: initiation into adepthood and further stages of progression through initiation and certification, annual professional certification for practitioners to uphold the quality of services provided, apprenticeships, and ongoing trainings at all levels.

Modern Mystery School Modalities

This is an overview of the modalities from the lineage of King Salomon that are cited in this book. These modalities are taught and certified by The Modern Mystery School. This is not an exhaustive list of all of the modalities and classes offered by The Modern Mystery School. For more information on classes and healings, please visit The Modern Mystery School website at www.modernmysteryschooint.com

Life Activation: a DNA activation that brings in more light, awakens your divine blueprint, and strengthens your connection with your Higher Self. The Life Activation brings more awareness of your gifts and true purpose. It helps release unconscious and genetic karmic patterns.

Full Spirit Activation: a healing session that strengthens the connection with the soul, making life more enjoyable and vibrant. It awakens the Thalamus region of the brain, and the Pituitary and Pineal glands which heighten the soul's awareness of the physical experience.

Empower Thyself Initiation: a two-day workshop and adept initiation that enters you into the lineage of King Salomon. It delivers ancient metaphysical teachings and tools to use in your daily life. Upon receiving the initiation, you have access to 10 times more light energy to manifest the life of your dreams.

Emotional Cord Cutting & Spell Removal: a healing that disconnects you from energetic cords to another person that are draining your energy. It frees up the energy to be used for positive things, leaving you feeling freer and more refreshed. The spell removal takes out negative energy from the third eye chakra. The emotional cord cutting is also referred to in this book as "Aura Clearing."

Ensofic Ray Treatments: a healing that is typically provided in three sessions which brings in the pure ray of energy from the Universe. It lifts away negative energies from the body, invigorates the physical body, and elevates your vibration above the lower vibrations of illness.

Etheric Reconstruction: a healing that focuses on the etheric part of the human energy system to restore our connection with the divine and celestial powers. It heals specific parts of the etheric structure: auric, magnetic, astral and dharmic body systems.

Galactic Activation: a two-day workshop and activation that awakens you to your potential as a galactic being. It activates the last two DNA strands out of 24 that cannot be activated with the Life Activation: the Galactic Code and the Divinity Code.

Healer's Academy: a five-day intensive course that trains and certifies a person to become a Life Activation Practitioner - someone who can do the Life Activation for others. A person can choose to attend Healer's Academy after they receive the Life Activation and attend Empower Thyself Initiation.

Isis Healing: a healing that facilitates the complete death and rebirth of the emotional body, using the energies of the Egyptian gods and goddesses Isis, Osiris, Geb and Nut. The client has more energy, vitality and brain capacity after the session.

Spark of Life: one of the most powerful remote/distance healings available. The practitioner accesses the divine spark to flow light to the client for healing of the physical, mental, and spirit bodies.

Spiritual Drug Detox Series: a healing series that is specific to a recovering addict of substance abuse. It heals the root of substance abuse on the spiritual and soul levels.

Universal Hermetic Ray Kabbalah: a 10-month ascension program that helps us know ourselves better as divine beings and strengthens our connection with God. We study the Tree of Life and take a journey into our thoughts, emotions, actions, and patterning to create a more fulfilling and joyful life.

Resources

The Modern Mystery School
The official contact for The Modern Mystery School international. From the website you may find a Certified Guide, Healer, Teacher, or Life Activation Practitioner near you.

www.modernmysteryschoolint.com
info@modernmysteryschoolint.com
1-877-275-1383

41 International Blvd.
Etobicoke, ON Canada, M9W 6H3

Mystery Teachings on Gaia TV
A Gaia original TV series hosted by Modern Mystery School international instructor, Dr. Theresa Bullard. Dr. Bullard has a Ph.D. in Physics. In this series she bridges the gap between science and spirituality and delves deep into metaphysical concepts.

www.mysteryteachings.com

Printed in the United States
by Baker & Taylor Publisher Services